From Dust to Glory

From Dust to Glory

The story of J. L. Tucker, Founder of
"The Quiet Hour" Broadcast

by L. E. TUCKER

A Sceptre Book
A Division of Royal Publishers
Nashville

Copyright © 1979 by *The Quiet Hour*

All rights reserved under International and Pan-American Conventions. Published in Nashville, Tennessee, by Thomas Nelson Inc., Publishers and simultaneously in Don Mills, Ontario, by Thomas Nelson & Sons (Canada) Limited. Manufactured in the United States of America.

Library of Congress Cataloging in Publication Data

Tucker, La Verne E   1922–
  From dust to glory.

  "A Sceptre book."
  "Writings of J. L. Tucker":
  1. Tucker, Julius Lafayette, 1895–   2. Seventh-Day Adventists —
Clergy—Biography.   3. Clergy—United States—Biography.   4. Quiet
hour (Radio program)
I. Title.
BX6193.T8T82   286'.73 [B]   79-22517
ISBN 0-8407-5699-2

To my loving wife, Alma, and our three sons, Bill, Don, and John.

CONTENTS

Preface

God has thrilling plans for everyone on planet Earth. God loves each one so much that He accepted the gracious offer of His only begotten Son to die in man's place, making it possible for every man, woman, and child to have everlasting life—if they would only accept this great salvation.

One of my father's favorite expressions of this truth is worded this way, "He raiseth up the poor out of the dust, and lifteth up the beggar from the dunghill, to set them among princes, and to make them inherit the throne of glory" (1 Sam. 2:8). It is Christ who lifts from the dust and brings a person to glory.

With this fact in mind, the title of this book was chosen. As each chapter in the life of my father unfolds, it is the hope of the author that renewed faith in this mighty God will be rekindled and that all who read shall not only know this ultimate experience but shall inspire others to know the joy of being lifted from the dust and set upon His throne.

About three months following the completion of

this manuscript my mother went to sleep in Jesus on August 9, 1979. She now awaits the call of the Life-giver on that resurrection morning. Her zeal for the work of God knew no bounds. Like the apostle Paul of old she was always willing to spend and be spent.

Ida Jane Tucker had a living relationship with her God. She loved her church. She gave sixty two years of full service to this glorious message. To see souls come into this truth was her chief delight. To see her son and grandsons faithfully carrying the torch of truth was one of her greatest joys. For this she lived and prayed.

The blessed hope has always been her joy and goal. She rests from her labors, but her influence lives on in the lives of many.

L. E. Tucker
Associate Speaker
The Quiet Hour

1

From Here to the World

Welcome! Come right on in—into our lives and into our love. Thanks so much for your interest in my father and his ministry. Today, Daddy (a term he still prefers I use) is a sprightly eighty-four-years-young. He can be found almost every day at our Redlands, California, headquarters, still shepherding *The Quiet Hour* ministry that he began half his life ago. Before we reveal the events that led him to where he is today, however, I know he would like for you to have a personally guided tour of his "home" at *The Quiet Hour* building.

As you drive up to our headquarters, I think you might agree that the name *The Quiet Hour* is well chosen. The one-story, beige block building stands at the corner of Brookside and Center, both broad boulevards on the western edge of this California town. Seven palm trees, reaching perhaps fifty feet in the air, line the sidewalk, giving shade to an immaculately kept green lawn. Notice our sign: Home of *The Quiet Hour* radio broadcast and *Search* telecast.

Now, walk through the glass door entrance. On your left is a guest book. We'd love to have a record of your visit, so won't you please sign in? On your right are some small, attractively printed booklets that we have written for *The Quiet Hour* listeners. Feel free to help yourself.

Up ahead we shall be walking through a large work area where twenty-two members will be going about the behind-the-scenes business necessary to make *The Quiet Hour* ministry possible. You will see that those in one corner are opening mail and separating it into bins, one for each state. The staff then counts the letters in each bin and keeps a record of the origin of the mail response. At this point, our readers begin the task of carefully going through each letter, noting requests for booklets or sermons, removing any contribution, and writing down prayer requests.

Once the readers are finished, our mail processors take over, performing whatever task is indicated. See those rows of cases along the wall? Those cases hold the name plates of 110,000 regular and casual correspondents to *The Quiet Hour*. Perhaps your name is among them. On the back of each plate is a record of support the listener has sent in over the years. The plates corresponding to the letters received for each particular work day are pulled from the trays and taken to a receipting area.

Here the plates are used individually to stamp the receipt, the mailing envelope, the return envelope, and any address label that may be required to send out literature, cassettes, or Bible correspondence courses.

Only after all the mail is handled in this fashion are the plates returned to the cabinets.

But the work is by no means finished! People must be sent letters thanking them for their gifts. Come into our Word Process area. Two IBM system six machines—a model 450 and 442—are quietly humming away to record the names and addresses of the letter writers. This information will be integrated into a letter of appreciation that is electronically typed by other pieces of IBM equipment. This same equipment is used in correspondence with the more than 450 radio stations that currently broadcast *The Quiet Hour* and the 60 television stations carrying the *Search* telecast.

Let's go through a door off the mail work area. Here you are in an office where the staff deals with the radio and TV stations. Ron Smith, manager of station relations and coordinator of missions projects, will point out a looseleaf volume that contains all the current station information, such as the call letters, locations, power, frequency on the dial or TV channel, the time *The Quiet Hour* is broadcast and *Search* telecast released, the date the program began on the station, and the weekly cost of air time. Each day stations may be added or dropped from the schedule, so this book is constantly updated.

Back again in the general work area, you'll notice three large information bulletin boards containing a variety of data. On the first is a large map of the United States. Hundreds of black pins scattered about the map indicate smaller stations carrying *The Quiet Hour*.

Thirty-six red pins point to large fifty-thousand-watt stations that are heard over a large geographic area.

Another symbol is a small representation of the famous praying hands art work. You will note these dotting the map on the upper West Coast and stretching along the northern tier of states and several Canadian provinces, then others affixed to points in Illinois, Ohio, Minnesota, and Pennsylvania. If you pause to count them, you will learn that currently some sixty stations are carrying the *Search* telecast.

Over here, on this second bulletin board, is an area devoted to the farflung missionary outreach of *The Quiet Hour*. Here is a map of the world with strings running out from Redlands to the far points of the globe where airplanes (supplied by readers of *The Quiet Hour Echoes* and listeners of *The Quiet Hour*) have been sent to aid in the spread of the gospel. The first aircraft went out to New Guinea in 1965. Since then, more than fifty others have been sent to such places as Korea, the Philippines, Borneo, the Solomon Islands, the New Hebrides, to Central and South America, to Canada and Alaska, and to Tanzania, Kenya, Ethiopia, Zaire, and Zambia.

This board also reveals that *The Quiet Hour* listeners have been actively engaged in projects such as building jungle chapels, sponsoring evangelistic meetings, and supplying missionaries with such hardware items as jeeps, trucks, vans, tractors, motorcycles, and bicycles. In 1978 for example, there were more than eighty-seven different missionary projects and more than $670,000 sent out to advance the cause of Adventist missionary work.

Let's look at this third bulletin board. Here are photographs taken during the forty-two years that *The Quiet Hour* has been on the air—pictures taken in Portland, Oregon, where the broadcast began, and then from where it continued in Oakland, California, and Berrien Springs, Michigan, and finally from the current headquarters in Redlands.

This next room we are entering is the room where *The Quiet Hour Echoes* is prepared for the printer. Out in the general workroom, that fellow you see sitting at the typewriter is Fred Rinker. He is answering the theological questions our listeners send in. The lovely lady next to him is my wife, Alma, whose responsibility is to oversee the work of the Bible correspondence school.

Over there is Carol Weaver, our office manager, who has been with *The Quiet Hour* for more than twenty years. She operates the Compugraphic typesetting equipment that provides photocopy for *The Echoes* and all the hundreds of booklets and books that are published by the broadcast.

Let's proceed to the studio and technical facilities used to record *The Quiet Hour*. To our left are four tape recorders that can be operated remotely from the broadcast studio itself, making the work of an engineer unnecessary. Three of these contain the opening theme of *The Quiet Hour*, the musical numbers, musical bridges and closing theme; while the other tape recorder is used to make the master recording.

You are fortunate enough to visit the headquarters building during a time when a recording of *The Quiet Hour* is taking place! If you look through the glass window, you will see Pastor J. L. Tucker seated to the far side at the microphone. If you will excuse me for a moment, I'll take that seat on his left so that I can manage the controls, watch the time clock, participate in the program, and pace it so it comes out exactly twenty-nine minutes and thirty seconds in length.

Now that the recording session is over, I'd like to show you the duplicating room so that you can see the master tape we just made re-recorded on four "slave" tape recorders. Although tapes are played on the air at seven and a half inches per second, here they are duplicated at a high speed of sixty inches per second. This saves a lot of time, since 450 programs have to be recorded each week to be sent out two at a time to stations carrying the broadcast. Programs are normally made at least five weeks in advance of being aired on the stations.

Around the corner from this room is the mailing and shipping room, which handles not only the sending out of tapes but also of books, booklets, cassettes, and other items that listeners request as well. Hundreds of orders are processed each day; and, typically, fifty thousand to one hundred thousand booklets go out to the post office each work day. Now that's a lot of mail!

Finally, here is the warehouse where an A. B. Dick 360 offset press handles small printing jobs. Also, those boxes you've spotted contain millions of *Quiet Hour* booklets and *The Quiet Hour Echoes*, which are printed outside our facilities.

But your tour of *The Quiet Hour* headquarters building will not be complete unless you have an opportunity to look into the office of Pastor Tucker, who just might be there since he works mornings and late afternoons most days. Looking to your left you might enjoy the mural, some seven by twenty feet in size, depicting the ministry of airplanes that *The Quiet Hour Echoes* readers and *The Quiet Hour* listeners have sent out to mission fields. To our right is a pleasant view through large, plate-glass windows that allow us to look out over the palm trees. Yes, that is my father's desk, which he freely admits is not always tidy. In truth, it is always covered with all kinds of letters, notes, and various items pertaining to the broadcast. What's this? A little marble sign that reassures us: "A cluttered desk is the sign of genius."

On a typical day, Pastor Tucker will be busy conferring with staff members, making telephone calls, and dictating replies to anywhere from 25 to 100 letters. We must have come in during one of those times he has slipped out of his office to work in his garden, which is located to the rear of the parking lot behind our building. Perhaps he will give you a tour of his forty-by-eighty feet plot containing turnips, tomatoes, peppers, cucumbers, eggplant, five rows of sweet corn, a strawberry patch that needs weeding, hubbard squash, spinach, and nine rows of raspberries.

As your tour of *The Quiet Hour* building concludes, perhaps you would like to know more about the man behind this ministry. How did he become the person he is, and how did his broadcast work grow from such a small beginning to be of such major proportions?

I'm glad you asked! As his son, it is my privilege to tell you the story of my father, J. L. Tucker, in this volume, *From Dust to Glory*.

2
The Twig Is Bent

"Back in the early days, what were the nationalities of people living in your part of South Dakota?" an old native of that area was asked.

"Well," he replied, touching his beard, "there were some French people. And some Swedish people. And then there were Tuckers!"

The Tuckers had migrated from England in the early 1870s to settle in the Civil Bend area near Elk Point. Thomas and Marianne Tucker raised a large family of one daughter and six boys, including Ernest.

As a young man, Ernest followed his father's occupation of farming but found time to use an ox hitched to a cart to court a pretty girl named Cora. Although they themselves were not religious, they were married by one of the great pioneers of the Seventh-day Adventist Church, Joshua V. Himes.

Ernest and Cora rented a small, second house that stood behind the main dwelling in Elk Point, and there they began their family. After the birth of their sons, Clayton and Ward, the young couple hoped that their third child would be a girl. But God had other plans. On April 5, 1895, He sent them yet another son, whom they named Julius Lafayette.

One detail of my father's birth stands out in his memory even now: "Folks told me that I made so much noise crying so loud that my grandfather declared this new baby would most certainly become an evangelist or a preacher."

A son rather than a daughter, nevertheless, came as a disappointment to the young mother. Not surprisingly, she pressed him into Jacob-like chores that normally might have been performed by a girl. "I was housebroken, taught to do the dishes, make the beds, clean the house, cook and do washing, churn the cream, and gather the eggs. At least it was good training for later years when my own home was established," my father remarks.

Through his long years of ministry, my daddy has often heard young people tell of their godly parents, regular family worship, and consistent examples set before them. Daddy didn't have that; and, in a sense, he feels he missed something vital.

It was not that his parents were bad. They were just average, worldly people who did not give the Lord Jesus a rightful place in their hearts. Though he often hungered for the memory of his name being mentioned in his mother's or father's prayers, this never occurred. They did not pray.

If there was any spiritual dimension in the Tucker household to be detected at all, it must have taken place — in God's providence—during the time his mother was carrying Julius in her womb.

The Twig Is Bent

To this day, Daddy is convinced that the prenatal experiences play an important part in shaping the attitudes and tendencies of the child. He is fond of quoting random lines from *Patriarchs and Prophets:*

God had an important work for the promised child of Manoah to do, and it was to secure for him the qualifications necessary for this work that the habits of both the mother and the child were to be carefully regulated . . . The child will be affected for good or for evil by the habits of the mother. She must herself be controlled by principle and must practice temperance and self-denial . . . if she would seek the welfare of her child.

"Every woman about to become a mother, whatever her surroundings, should encourage constantly a happy, contented disposition, knowing that for all her efforts in this direction she will be repaid tenfold in the physical as well as the moral character of her offspring," Daddy stresses.

While my father was still a little fellow, his parents drove a covered wagon from Elk Point hundreds of miles south to settle in Beeville, Texas. After plowing the ground and killing forty rattlesnakes, Julius' father was going to show those Texans how to raise forty acres of cotton. But he learned a few things from them, too—mainly that cotton farming was a hard life. When it came time to pick the crop, Julius was given his own cotton bag. "I doubt I added much to the income," he says.

After two years, the family decided that South Dakota hadn't been so bad after all and began the long trek north. But it hadn't been a total loss, at least not for a mother who could see the funnier side of things. "Mother used to tease my dad by saying he had gypsy blood, that he was itchy, and that he was a rolling stone who could always see greener pastures somewhere else."

Those eyes soon looked westward and father Ernest decided to homestead in Lewistown, Montana. Only this time, they would go not by wagon but by train. There were no dining cars in those days, so Julius' mother cooked a mountain of food for the trip. It was a good thing she did because when the journey was less than halfway completed, a heavy snow began to fall and soon turned into a blizzard. Before long, the raging snow had covered the tracks to a depth of several feet, halting the train's progress.

The train crew did their best to keep the chilly passengers calm, if not comfortable, during the long hours of the night. Some dried fruit and crackers were brought in from the baggage car, and Mrs. Tucker's food was passed around so far as it went. Finally, a relief engine with a big snowplow managed to open the track and drag the marooned train back to civilization and safety.

It was all great fun for an eight-year-old boy. Julius even enjoyed the three-week wait in a Chinese-operated hotel, which ended when the snow melted and their journey could be resumed.

Back in those days, Lewistown was the end of the railroad. From that point, the old-fashioned stagecoaches, with their great leather springs and usually drawn by four horses, provided the means of transportation to the mining towns beyond. Julius loved to catch on behind one of these and ride a few blocks through the dusty streets. He was thrilled beyond words when a kindly driver would let him ride up in the high seat beside him.

Daddy recalled his stagecoach experiences to fashion an illustration he sometimes uses in his sermons. It seemed that on one of these lines it was possible for passengers to buy either a first, second, or third class ticket. A wealthy man from the East wanted to visit a gold mine in which he owned stock.

"Do you want to go first, second, or third class?" asked the driver.

"Nothing but the best. First class, of course," he replied.

Another approached the driver a little later, and seeing what the first man had paid, inquired what the second class passage would cost. He was informed that it was about half of the first class fare, and he decided to take it.

Then a miner returning to his work asked for a third class ticket and paid about half of the second class fare.

When the driver hollered, "All aboard!" all classes of riders got into the same coach, all having the same type of seats and the same comfort. As the horses galloped along, the wealthy Easterner pondered how he had been taken in by these Westerners. So did the second class passenger.

Their meditations on how they had been cheated were rudely interrupted when the driver, after traveling several miles from the town, brought his four horses to a stop at the base of a long, steep hill.

"First class passengers, keep your seats," the driver

shouted down from above. "Second class passengers, get out and walk. Third class passengers, get out and push."

My daddy grins. "On the gospel coach, we're all riding third class. God expects everyone of us to push, to do his best. Jesus says He has given to every man his work."

My father remembers Lewistown, not only for this illustration, but for another reason — for its wide-open gambling and twenty-one saloons. One of his twice-daily chores in those early days was to buy and bring home a gallon of beer for the family to drink, although he, himself, never liked it.

Still, the frontier city provided much excitement. "On weekends, cowboys and miners would come into town, drink a lot, gamble a lot, and get into brawls and shootings. What devilment we kids—a bunch of roughnecks—got into almost every day. It was only by the mercy of God that we didn't land in reform school," Daddy says.

The homestead the family filed for became only a house, never a home. They lived in a one-room, sixteen-by-thirty feet dwelling. Although a lovely spring of fine water flowed nearby, it failed to bring a refreshing hope that their stay would be permanent. After four years, the Tuckers, one by one, migrated back to South Dakota, with Julius being the first to go. He lived with his grandmother, who was known for her home remedies. When the boy picked up a skin disease, grandmother went into action by plastering him with sulphur and molasses. The mixture worked.

When at last the family reassembled, they rented a

small acreage and lived again in a one-room house. Julius slept on the floor with corn husks in a bag for a mattress. But gradually they prospered and were able to purchase the old Tucker home. The deed stated that the land ran "down to the river" (the Missouri River). Sometimes the channel would suddenly change and add acres of rich land to their farm. Then, just as suddenly, the channel would shift again; and the river would take back what it had given.

By this time, Julius had entered his early teens and was already beginning to develop the deep, resonant voice that has characterized his radio ministry for so many decades. The voice was developed in a strange way. In his words, "As I brought the cows in from the pasture and milked them in the barn, I would sing to them. I wish I had a picture of myself seated on a stool, squirting some of the milk into the pail and some into the mouths of my pet dog, runt pig, and cat, all the while just singing away!"

It was good to be back near water again, near the Missouri River. However, that river almost became the means of the young boy's untimely death.

Twice each week, Julius and his father checked a fish trap that they had submerged in the river. This provided a good opportunity for a swim. On one of these occasions, two neighborhood girls also happened to be there and decided to cool off in the river. But they got into deep water where they were unable to touch bottom, panicked, and began to scream.

"You get Freda and I'll get Grace!" farmer Tucker shouted to his son. Instead of running up the bank to extend aid to the girl, Julius jumped into the water and tried to swim upstream. Finally, he reached the floundering girl, who promptly grabbed him by the neck and took them both under water.

My father recalls, "Underneath I got untangled from her arm around my neck, all the time trying to make our way to shallow water, but we went under again. At last, my father, having rescued the other girl, was able to grab our arms and legs and pull us to safety as we clung to each other in desperation."

For a while, Julius lay unconscious on the bank, but slowly he began to breathe again. Later, when he was able to laugh about the incident, he asked the young lady, "Why don't you love me on the land like you did in the water?"

While one romance may have failed, another had a humorous side to it. Julius was attracted to one of the town girls who expressed some loyalty to him by doing battle on his behalf. "Some of the other boys jumped me one time—three of them," he recalls. "They had me down in the dirt. Then, this little lady took her hat pin out of her hair and went after those fellows until she had them on the run. They never tackled me again when she was around."

Many years before the invention of radio or television , what was a boy to do during the long hours of loneliness? Julius found the answer in books. His mother had once been a school teacher and had retained a great interest in reading.

"Mother would go down with us to the riverbank in the wintertime, and we'd cut a lot of wood with a view to sawing and selling it. She loved to read novels aloud, and she had a beautiful voice for doing it. She would read to us from a novel while sitting on the saw buck. I'd be on one end of the long crosscut saw and one of my brothers on the other. Not only would she read to us when we were working out-of-doors, but later in our home during the winter evenings.''

Reading cheap novels was a habit that my daddy would have to struggle to break as an adult. But he began a certain withdrawal process while still in his teens.

''One night along about eleven or twelve, I was reading *The Sorrows of Satan.* All of a sudden, an electric storm hit. I was sitting in the dining room at the table when a great ball of fire moved slowly right through the screen, through the open door, and right around where I was sitting. I watched it go out into the kitchen and exit through the open door.

''My father was roused from his sleep because of the roar of the thunder, and he came out to ask me what the trouble was. I told him what I had seen and that it had scared me to death. So I never did finish reading *The Sorrows of Satan!*''

Daddy had learned to read in a public school about a mile from his house. Mr. Rhodes was master of the one-room school that contained all eight grades. One day, when perturbed at something Julius had forgotten, he placed his hand on the boy's hair and kind of pulled it in a playful way.

''Julius,'' he said to Daddy, ''you have a memory as long as a toad's tail.''

Daddy got to thinking about all the toads he had

seen. They didn't have any tails. He says, "I learned quite early that my memory was short, but how patient those teachers were with me!"

Although Daddy would be handicapped with a poor memory throughout his life, God still chose to use him in His service. He was soon to set out on that lifetime calling.

3
New Directions

Although the father and mother of Julius were not themselves religious, they endeavored to have their children attend the local Sabbath school and Adventist church, which was about a mile down the road from the Tucker's home.

Sometimes Daddy got more out of church attendance than he had bargained for—like the time a temperance meeting was held. My father thought it was a good idea to pledge himself to refrain from the use of tobacco and liquor. But before he signed the pledge, someone penciled in the additional stipulation against the use of tea or coffee. Yet, he never regretted making this commitment. "From that day to this, to my knowledge I have never drunk a cup of tea or coffee. I think I am better off, healthwise, for it."

One of the great experiences that changed his young life occurred when the president of the denomination's area conference, Pastor C. M. Babcock, came to town to hold revival meetings. Julius attended each service, never missing a night. When a baptismal class was organized, he joined it. He remembers walking down with others to be baptized in the Missouri River, the place where once he had almost drowned.

Daddy remembers this as the most wonderful experience he had ever had. A dozen or more waded out one by one into the shallow water to confess their faith in Christ. As church members on shore sang, "I Will Follow Thee My Savior," Julius was baptized into Christ and became a member of the church.

A few days after Julius' baptism, Elder Babcock came out to the tomato cannery where Julius was working and began to talk. Then he came to the point of his visit: "Julius, I think God wants you to become a preacher."

Daddy couldn't have been more stunned. He thought of his timidity, of how he was afraid even to sing in the choir. Any type of public ministry scared him. Not surprisingly, the young, teen-age boy gave a Sarah and Abraham laugh, doubting that God could work such a miracle in his life.

Babcock repeated his statement, this time more emphatically: "Yes, I think God wants you to be a preacher."

"Well," the boy replied, "I can't go away to school. My folks need me here. I'm sort of the head of the farm." He went on to explain that his older brothers had married and moved away. Working the farm fell principally on his shoulders.

"But if I can get your folks to consent to it," the pastor continued, "will you go? As chairman of the school board, I can get you a job so that you can work your way through."

Julius thought for a moment. He knew very well that his parents would say no. So he felt confident in replying, "Yes, I will."

Wanting to seize the brand while it was still hot, Pastor Babcock walked with Julius over to his parents' home and asked if he could speak with them.

"Mr. and Mrs. Tucker, I want to talk to you about something very important. But before I do, I think we ought to talk to God."

The memory of that scene is still vivid in my daddy's mind. "This is the only time I had ever seen my father and mother on their knees. That preacher had a way of getting right up into the throne room of the Eternal. I began to get nervous as I opened my eyes and took a peek at father and saw tears in his eyes. I looked over at mother, and the tears were running down her cheeks. When we got up from prayer, before I could say a word to change the trend of things, my father spoke.

" 'Well, if Julius wants to be a preacher, it's all right with us. We can get along and hire somebody in the busy time.' Mother volunteered that she could do more of the chores."

That very summer, life as a farm boy came to an end for Julius. He would study for the ministry.

The Plainview Academy, located in Redfield, South Dakota, was a small boarding school of perhaps 150 students. True to his word, Pastor Babcock got Julius a job as a janitor. "I scrubbed more floors and cleaned more blackboards than anybody else . . . and I loved it."

Even though matriculation costs were low and a

dollar was a dollar back in those days, Julius felt the need to earn more money; so he returned to what he knew best, working in the fields.

"I was a good corn picker," Father recalls. "I wasn't lazy. A hundred bushels a day was just routine, and if I pushed myself I could even hit 120 or 125. The most I ever picked in one day was 132 bushels."

It was hard work pulling off the ears from the stalks and throwing them up in the air to bounce off the "bangboard," a term probably unknown to most city dwellers. Father explains, "The bangboard was located on the far side of a wagon. I would throw up the ears, and they would hit the bangboard and then drop back into the wagon.

"One day while working, I heard two ears hit the bangboard at the same time. I knew I was good, but I knew I wasn't *that* good. Two ears at a time? I looked up and saw Pastor Babcock."

He had seen the industrious young man working hard at his job and had asked who he was. When informed that the worker was Julius Tucker, the pastor walked out and spent the rest of the late afternoon in conversation.

"That was the only sermon of his I remember," Daddy says. "He took a real interest in me, not just because I was somebody he had baptized, but because he wanted to."

Many years later Daddy was able to return the favor, in part, by performing the second wedding ceremony for Babcock, who had been widowed.

Appropriately enough, Julius joined the ministerial

class, very much afraid that it would mean speaking in public. It did. He tells it best in his own words:

They asked different members of the class to take the chapel service. I took as my theme an incident from the life of David when he was keeping his father's sheep on the back side of the desert. The Bible says, ". . . and there came a lion . . ." (1 Sam. 17:34). I told how David rushed over there and did battle with him. He killed the lion and saved the sheep.

My knees were hitting together loudly, and the mist came over my eyes, and my brain became a blank. When I came to, I had finished and had taken my seat. Only it wasn't my seat. I was sitting beside some young lady. I never took that text—"and there came a lion"—again for many years. But how I love it now.

Perhaps it is not surprising that a minister present in chapel that day said, "Don't bother with Julius Tucker. He will never make a preacher."

But some could see beyond the rough edges of this farm boy and recognize a potential that could be tapped and trained. One of the older men of the conference committee said, "Let Tucker come with me." "Tuckie" is what he actually called him. Together they spent part of the summer holding meetings, selling literature, talking to all who would listen. It was a great experience.

Julius enjoyed dormitory life, soon learning what was allowed and what wasn't. Although the young men and women were largely kept separate, some daring ones tried to cross the boundaries and "mingle" illegally. One day a friend of Julius' (a fellow with an artificial limb) sneaked over to the girls' side. When he heard the matron, or "preceptress" as she was called, coming in, he hurriedly dived under the girl's bed. But he failed to get his wooden leg completely out of sight.

"Peggedy, what are you doing under there?" the matron demanded.

There was no response.

"I'll try again—what are you doing under there?"

The boy thought quickly and came up with what he thought was a justifiable excuse. "Just meditating, ma'am."

Julius, himself, was meditating about someone else at this time—someone who seemed to him to be the most charming girl in all the world.

4

Ida

Of the many girls who attended Plainview Academy, one had special qualities that made her stand out. Daddy remembers:

We fellows would get together to talk about all the different girls. Ida Stratton would come up in the conversation, and we'd all agree that there was just no chance of any of us ever marrying her. She made a great impression on us. She possessed a certain dignity, an aloofness. She was not like some of the others. Yet, I insisted that if the right one ever came along, she'd fall just like the rest of them because she had a heart like everyone else.

Ida had been born to a poor South Dakota farm family on March 18, 1892. Her father was irreligious and even opposed the preaching of the gospel. But her mother was different. Originally a Baptist, she had become a Seventh-day Adventist after reading their publication the *Signs of the Times*. She was determined that any children born to her would be brought up in the nurture and admonition of the Lord.

That instruction found a ready reception in Ida. Her mother observed that the young girl had "always had a religious turn" and was greatly interested in Christian things. A colporteur (one who sells religious books door-to-door) visiting the farm from time to time suggested that the girl might some day be engaged in Christian outreach.

Perhaps music would also be a part of some future ministry, Ida thought. On her own, the young girl learned to play the piano at her grandmother's house. She had a zither with the names of the keys marked on it. She wrote the names of the corresponding keys on the piano for self-instruction. She felt the Lord helped her not only to play well but to sing also.

Ida attended the Seventh-day Adventist academy in Redfield, South Dakota; then, after moving to New Mexico, she began to teach church school. Back once again in her native state, she learned that she had a love for colporteur work. With horse and buggy, she traveled from one farm to another and proved to be the best salesperson in the state. Why was she so successful? "I prayed a lot and the Lord was with me."

The reward for her good work was a scholarship to Plainview Academy and the position of teacher in the grade school.

One day, Ida was sitting with a girl friend, waiting for chapel service to begin, when in walked a handsome youth with black, wavy hair.

"Who is that young man who just came in?" she turned and asked her friend.

"Oh, that's Julius Tucker. He's one of the finest fellows you'd ever hope to meet."

Ida was impressed with his manner and the way he carried himself, tall and stately. She had no idea that they would soon begin an association that was to last more than sixty-five years.

Before long, Julius began to notice Ida. Since he was the custodian of the institution, he had the right to go anywhere he wished. He soon found himself going with increasing frequency to the section of the building where Ida was teaching church school.

Life at Plainview Academy consisted mainly of chapel services and classes. When the lake froze over, as it soon did when winter began, the students would go there for ice skating. Often the couples would hold hands as they glided over the surface. But Ida was known as one who couldn't be easily touched.

But that didn't keep Julius from trying! "I remember once skating together, and I got to hold her hand. I thought it was a miracle. Even though we wore gloves, I felt something tingling all over," Daddy says.

On another occasion, after they had become better acquainted, he tried again to hold her hand. But she slowly pulled it away. Again, he reached out.

"Why do you want to hold my hand?" she asked at last.

"Because I like you."

"Oh, is that all? Well, they all like me."

That wasn't the remark of a proud person but of one who knew that affection had to be reserved for the one who would ultimately share her life. Ida had always believed that God had a special person chosen for her. She recognized, even as a young girl, that if the Lord ever wanted her to marry, somewhere that young man was alive and growing to manhood. "So I prayed for him, that the Lord would prepare him to fit into my life and prepare me to fit into his. And I knew that in His good time the Lord would bring us together."

Plainview Academy maintained certain conventions and regulations for those students who were romantically interested in each other. Normally, this would promote relationships. But for Julius and Ida, the agenda almost led to a permanent break-up.

Students could ask the matron for the privilege of visiting in the parlor. Instead of being objective about the young couple, the matron was absolutely convinced that Julius was not for Ida. Another boy, she thought, would make her a far better match. So the dean set about to torpedo the relationship—and she almost succeeded.

My mother recalls the incident vividly, even to this day:

Julius and I had agreed to meet in the parlor at a certain hour one afternoon. I got there first; and when I opened the door, I saw that the dean of women's twelve-year-old daughter, one of my pupils, was there. I didn't say a word but just closed the door. Pretty soon, I came back and looked in again. The girl was still there and acted as though she intended to stay. I had the feeling that Julius had been there and had seen her, too. Only I didn't know that he thought I had planted her there as a joke on him.

The dinner hour came, and Ida made her way to the dining hall and took a seat at a table. She joined the conversation and soon began laughing with the other students.

Just then, Julius walked in and looked right at her. He thought they were laughing at his predicament. He threw his head back and walked right past her into the kitchen.

"I wanted to reach out and grab him by the coattail," my mother remembers. "I could see the matron through the lattice work, and she was getting all kinds of fun out of this. But I couldn't do a thing, so I just sat there." She thought she would catch him after dinner and explain.

It was the custom, following a meal, for the students to stroll for a few minutes out on the lawn as the sun was setting. Ida walked outside and saw Julius. She began walking toward him, but he turned his back in rejection. He had vowed that no joke could be played on him.

Ida retreated to her school room and sat in the darkness. Maybe the matron was right, she thought. Maybe Julius was not the one for her.

After a while, dejected, she began to walk back to her dormitory. In the chilly darkness, she saw someone standing nearby. She knew who it was, but she was determined not to greet him. As she passed by, he reached out and took her gently by the arm. But she pulled away.

"Why did you treat me like that this evening?" Julius asked.

"And why don't you let me explain?"

She looked directly into his face and told him that the planting of the little girl in the parlor was not her idea and that she had not been laughing at him at the dinner table.

In a few hours, Julius was to leave school early to return home to help with the spring planting.

"May I see you a little while before I go?"

"Well, don't ask the matron," Ida warned.

Julius got permission from the principal of the academy to visit Ida that evening in her school room. They talked long into the night—so long, in fact, that Julius missed his train.

The next morning, as Ida walked down the stairs to breakfast, she looked out the window and saw a half dozen girls bidding goodbye to Julius as he was about to leave to catch a later train.

"But it didn't worry me," she recalls, "because I had said goodbye to him the night before, and that was enough!"

During the next two school years, Julius gradually saw more of Ida. But there came a day when she decided that the relationship must end. She had become interested in someone else. Finally, she told him, "I don't want to see you again because I don't want to hurt you. To tell you the truth, I like someone else better than I do you. To allow you to come and spend your time, to build up your hopes—I can't permit it."

My daddy was speechless, at first. But he soon found his voice. "Well, I'll take that chance. I'll take that chance." On that basis, she permitted him to continue seeing her.

One particular day stands out in both their memories. They planned an all-day picnic, just the two of them. They rode out to the Sioux River near Elk

Point and rented a boat for seventy-five cents for the day. While rowing along, they came to a tree covered with grape vines hanging out over the water to form a beautiful arbor. Julius thought this would be a good place to propose.

"I pulled the boat in there," Daddy relates. "We always took a book along to read so that if the conversation lagged we would have something spiritual to occupy our minds." It was their custom whenever dating to pray and ask God's blessing on their friendship.

"We were seated together in the boat, and I was reading aloud to Ida. She began to look into the book, and her face got closer and closer to mine. My heart began to pound so loud I was sure she must be able to hear it. Finally, I couldn't resist any longer. I turned and kissed her on the cheek."

She responded by slapping him and jumping up so quickly that she almost capsized the boat.

"I was kind of hoping that she'd fall in so I could rescue her," Daddy says, with a twinkle in his eyes.

"I wanted Julius to know that I wasn't accepting kisses like that." Ida stormed out of the shaky boat and later climbed a tree. Daddy insists that he chased her up and refused to let her come down until she said yes to his proposal. He took a photograph of her perched on the limb of the tree, and he carries it with him to this day to show people whenever he relates the story.

Later, when they had publicly declared their engagement, the kisses came easier. As they would drive along the countryside, they would occasionally come to a covered bridge or to a place where the trees grew thickly over the road to form a kind of tunnel. "Then I'd kiss her," Daddy confesses. "And I would hope for tunnels."

They planned to work in two different counties in a colporteur ministry that summer and to marry in the fall. Julius went to Billings, Montana, to work by himself and to live with a pastor friend. He would go out on Monday mornings and spend the week canvassing the county and then return Friday afternoons for the Sabbath meeting.

The pastor was planning a big, evangelistic meeting using a tent. But the man who was supposed to help him put up the tent failed to show. The pastor called the conference president, who asked if some local person could be hired to help pitch the tent and be tentmaster.

"Well, I've got a young Plainview Academy student here by the name of Julius Tucker."

"Hire him," came the suggestion.

That solved the problem of help in connection with the tent. But who would play the organ?

"I know a young lady down at Livingston who plays the piano and organ and has had experience in tent meetings—and in Bible work, too," Daddy offered.

"Do you suppose she will come and help us?"

"I think so. Sure, if we ask her."

They did, and Ida agreed to come. The pastor paid them each six dollars per week for their labor.

Since they were already planning to get married that fall, the president of the conference, Elder George

Watson, suggested that to facilitate their ministry they should marry then. Julius and Ida didn't have to think about the matter for long before they agreed.

The only place they could conveniently live was in an auxiliary fourteen-by-sixteen feet tent pitched next to the main tent where the evening meetings were held. Ida curtained it off into three small rooms. Together they went to the local dime store and bought a table service for two and some utensils. At a second-hand store they purchased a bed, a dresser, a rocking chair, a little gatelegged table, and a two-burner stove. The remainder of their furniture they fashioned from orange crates.

Daddy almost missed the wedding. He had an errand downtown and rode his bicycle—but on the sidewalk instead of on the street. A policeman stopped him and threatened to arrest him as an example to other lawbreakers.

"Well, I'll let you go this time," the officer said at last. "But don't you ever do it again!" Daddy promised that he wouldn't.

Julius and Ida, along with five or six guests, gathered in Pastor Fred Cole's parsonage where he performed the brief ceremony. The day was July 4, 1917. Daddy is fond of saying that he lost his independence on Independence Day.

The day had been dark and overcast, with heavy showers. But just as the ceremony ended, the storm ceased and the sun came out and shone brightly. Both considered it a good sign.

Hand in hand, Mr. and Mrs. Julius Tucker walked

the mile from the pastor's house to find their first tent home. As they raised the flap and entered, they had no idea that someone else—an uninvited guest— would soon visit them in the middle of the night.

5
Moving Out

"I felt I had the world by the tail on a downhill pull," Daddy recalls of his tent honeymoon. "I was married to the girl of my heart, and I even had eighteen dollars in cash."

But that first Sunday night as he and his bride lay sleeping, someone crept inside and stole it all. They didn't have a dime in the world, and both were far from home.

Julius told the evangelist, who immediately called the conference office for help: "Tucker was robbed, sleeping on guard. Please send him a little money."

For the next two months, the young couple aided the evangelist in holding tent meetings at several locations in Billings. As tentmaster, Daddy would pass out the songbooks and lead the singing. When he couldn't hit a high note, Mother would do it for him and sing loudly enough for the two of them.

The man who had originally been scheduled to be tentmaster was also scheduled to be the dean of men at Mount Ellis Academy in Bozeman. Since Julius and

Ida had done such a good job in Billings, why should they not be sent as the missing man's replacement? At the beginning of the school year that September, they were on the job.

At age twenty-two, Daddy found himself the preceptor of a group of occasionally unruly young men—some of whom were older than he.

The challenge came the very first night. Daddy recalls the incident well.

There was one rascal who had driven away the previous dean of men. He had bragged to the others that he would get rid of me, too.

We had evening worship; when it was over, I told the boys pointedly, "Let's get right down to business. We are here to study and to learn, so go in and get started."

I dismissed them, and all the boys went into their rooms except this one fellow. He just stood there, defying me, knowing the others were waiting to see what would happen. I told him my suggestion to go inside included him.

"I'd like to see you make me," the boy replied.

Without so much as a pause, Daddy leaned his entire 190-pound frame against the lad and pushed him inside. Only then did the youngster realize that he was dealing with a different sort of dean. The president of the school ordered the boy to be expelled that very night, lest he make additional trouble in the future.

But not all of the discipline problems were so serious. The primitive school lacked a central heating system, so each boy had a stove in his room to keep him warm on the cold Montana nights. But some of the students used their stoves for forbidden purposes, such as frying eggs that they had taken from the hen house.

In addition to his duties as dean of men, Daddy taught history, mathematics, and Bible. "I really sweated, trying to keep ahead of the students in algebra. I got the answers to some of the problems on my knees." Ida taught in the church school nearby. They lived in one room of the boys' dormitory.

Although my father had only an eleventh-grade education, he found he could be an educator when forced into it or into some other avenue of service. To quote Daddy on the matter, "Everything I have done for the Lord, I have just been pushed into. But I had sense enough to stay with it. That's the only redeeming feature I have."

To do the work of an evangelist, especially in a non-Adventist area, required a certain type of persistence. The conference thought that Julius and Ida had it, so when school was out the following summer, they were asked to work in the northeastern Montana district. It's here that Daddy considers his real ministry to have started.

They went out with an elder preacher who had asked that the Tuckers be sent along with him. So away they went, as far as the Canadian line to such unknown cities as Plentywood and Dagmare.

In addition to his other duties, Daddy was assigned to preach Monday nights. On one occasion, the evangelist and his two newly married assistants visited a lady who remarked how much she enjoyed the preaching, especially on Monday nights.

When they left and entered the evangelist's old Ford to make another call, he turned and asked, "Tucker, what did I preach on last Monday?" Only then did he realize what Daddy had known all along—that it was his preaching that had been commended. This greatly encouraged my father.

Finally, Julius and Ida were sent off on their own to Scoby, Montana, "to sink or swim, to live or die, to survive or perish," as Daddy says. Scoby was not exactly a religious community. Only one Adventist lady lived there.

The best approach seemed to be to call in homes and to distribute copies of the *Signs of the Times*. It was a weekly publication in those days. When the first bundle of fifty *Signs* arrived, Julius was suddenly seized with "salesman's terror."

"I was afraid this was too much for me," Daddy recalls. "We went out looking at the formidable houses. I turned and suggested to Ida that we try the houses on the other side of town. We walked over there, but even those little shacks looked big. So we went to another part of the little town, and those houses looked bigger still." As Julius was about to suggest another street, Ida said, "We are going in here!"

They couldn't have made a better choice. Although the home belonged to an atheist, the lady of the house gave them a warm welcome and eagerly welcomed the religious publication. She'd have to hide it, she explained, because her husband would not allow her to have anything Christian in the home, not even a Bible.

The wife and children were forbidden to attend Sunday school.

The Tuckers went back to visit each week, fighting a battle that was no less real to them than World War I, which was raging across the sea.

"You know," Daddy told the lady one day, "I believe that if your husband would let me, I could show him from the Bible that Kaiser Bill can't win."

When her husband learned of the offer, the atheist declared, "Let that young upstart come over, and I'll hear him."

Daddy made a frantic study of Daniel 2 and came well-prepared to show that there would be only four worldwide kingdoms, according to Bible prophecy. He took Ida along for protection.

Daddy recalls that the man was very cold at the beginning of the study but warmed up gradually as it progressed. Then, he suddenly brought down his fist on the table where they were seated.

"Tucker, you're right! I see it! I see it!"

This first convert became the best and only advertising agency that Julius and Ida needed to promote their ministry in Scoby. "This young preacher knows his Bible from A to Z," the former unbeliever declared to those who gathered at the local post office to wait for the mail to come by train.

Before long, Bible studies had sprung up all over town. Soon they were able to organize a little Sabbath school of some thirty attenders—all this without officially preaching even one sermon.

To this day, Daddy makes a distinction between

the two types of outreach. "When I just talk to people, that's a Bible study. When I get up and pound a desk, that's a sermon."

Although licensed to preach, Julius was not yet ordained. So he asked the conference president to come up and baptize the converts. The visiting cleric was impressed with what the Tuckers had accomplished.

The young couple ministered physically as well as spiritually, for the year 1918 brought with it an influenza epidemic that took many lives. They stopped their home Bible studies and began to administer hydrotherapy treatments to those who had been stricken. Ida would use hot water and heavy clothes to warm the patients, then apply cold packs to drive in the heat and break up the disease. Julius would do the household and farmyard chores for the sick.

As the word spread, others asked these "angels of mercy" to come and minister to them. During those terrible months of sickness, the Tuckers lost only one patient, whose treatment was begun too late to save her.

People also died from other causes, of course, and Daddy well remembers his first two funerals. A Methodist parishioner had died, and Julius was asked to conduct the service in her pastor's absence. While returning from the cemetery, he felt compelled to talk to a young, teen-age girl who was visiting with another young girl who was living with the Tuckers. He discussed with her the brevity of life and the need to be ready for any eventuality. But she was not interested and cared not for this admonition. That night, this young girl and her mother were shot to death by an enraged uncle, who then turned the gun on himself. The following day, Daddy was asked to conduct a triple funeral.

"The text that came to my mind was Isaiah 39:4: 'What have they seen in thine house?' I asked myself what that young girl had seen in my house. Had I known what God knew, that this young life and the lives of the two others would soon end, would I have pressed the invitation of the Lord a little more than I did? This experience has been a challenge to me from that day to this," Daddy states.

The people of Scoby needed an ordained minister to work among them. At the next conference session, which lasted ten days, it was decided that my daddy be formally ordained. He had put in only two of the usually required three years of practical field experience. Nevertheless, the suggestion received a favorable reception and was accepted.

Daddy traveled to College Place, Washington, to be ordained along with eight other men, all of whom had had more education than he. He felt unworthy to be ordained because he knew his work would be a heavy responsibility for his young shoulders.

On his way home, Julius stopped in Helena, Montana, to visit an old retired preacher friend. The older man suggested that now that Julius was ordained he would be called upon to perform weddings. "Here's a copy of the ceremony I use," he volunteered.

As it turned out, the first thing Julius was called on to do when he reached home was to perform a wedding. It was one to remember!

"The girl was the eager part of it," says Daddy, "and I would not be surprised if she had done the proposing. I told the couple what we were going to do and how things were to go. I explained that at the close of the ceremony, following prayer, I would say, 'And now it gives me great joy to present to you Mr. and Mrs. So and So.' Later, at the actual ceremony, the moment I said 'amen,' the bride jumped up, grabbed the groom in her arms, and said, 'I gotcha! I gotcha!' My part of the ceremony was over."

Another thing Daddy learned while in Scoby was that the power of the Word of God, not the eloquence of the preacher's words, wins souls. "I was not eloquent, nor did I preach in those early days. I gave Bible studies and let God talk to people. They responded."

But he would be preaching soon in a regular pulpit ministry. And he was to discover that when it came to sermon preparation, two heads were better than one.

6
The Team

Since my mother was determined, even as a young girl, that she was going to marry a preacher (if she married at all), it seemed logical to her that she should be prepared to help him. She was impressed with the preaching of a certain Elder Haynes, and one day she asked him, "How do you write a sermon and fix it up?"

"Well, I choose my subject and look up references in the index to the *Spirit of Prophecy* to see what is written about it. I take the Scripture texts the various books suggest. Then I read all about it in six to ten books of the *Spirit of Prophecy* and build on it more and more.* Then I find several other sources and write those down, too."

My, isn't that wonderful! Ida thought. *I could learn to do that.*

Before long she tried her hand. My mother prepared

*The *Spirit of Prophecy* is a multi-volume work written by one of the founders of the Seventh-day Adventists.

a sermon on the theme of the investigative judgment for my daddy to preach. And many years later when I was a sophomore theology student at Walla Walla College, my father asked me to speak at his church in Portland, Oregon, and I was faced with preparing my first sermon. My mother told me that if she could be of any help she was ready to give it. And she did. She helped me prepare the same sermon she had written out for my father two decades before. I preached it proudly and told the audience of its origin.

Since Daddy had had so little formal training, he welcomed the sermonic assistance. "Ida would help me study, and we would make an outline together. She would do some research in the few books that constituted our library and then write out the sermon.

"When she had a page written, I would take it out behind the woodshed and commit it to memory. By the time I had finished, she would have another page ready for me." Daddy insists that it has never been easy for him to memorize. He declares that even without a brilliant mind, however, he was able to convey the intended thoughts and was well-prepared for delivering his sermons.

Word of this unorthodox approach to sermon preparation got around. An old preacher, not known for excellent pulpit work, said to Julius, "Well, I don't have my wife writing out my sermons for me!" *No*, my father thought to himself, *but you should.*

Daddy praises the help his young wife provided. "If I didn't do well on some occasions, Ida would encourage me. 'It was fine, good. You made a mistake or two, but you won't make them again.'

"At first, Ida would sit on the front pew with her eyes fastened on me during my sermons to see if I left anything out. But finally she got to where she would take a little nap on me, and I took this as a compliment. She figured I was going to get through the sermon all right, and she didn't have to stay awake to make sure."

Mother also helped in those early years of ministry by playing the piano at all the services, at least until the children were born. But even her aid had its limits, particularly the time her husband was erroneously billed as a singing evangelist!

"I couldn't sing," Daddy insists, "but I had to try. I suffered humiliation and stage fright. If a man could earn salvation by suffering, I had it coming."

Finally, their ministry in Scoby concluded, my parents moved to Lewistown, Montana, again to do pioneering work. This time they used a different approach. They rented a hall in which to hold evangelistic meetings.

It was there, after five years of marriage, that they awaited the birth of their first child. When the baby seemed overdue, they journeyed by train to Missoula to consult a well-known Adventist physician named Thornton. There, on April 24, 1922, they welcomed a boy, whom they named LaVerne. He, of course, was I. And two years later, on May 19, my sister, Jewell, joined us to complete the family of four.

It was about this time the Lord spoke to my father about the matter of reading cheap novels, a practice he had begun years before while growing up. Daddy tells it best:

Even after I became a preacher, I was still reading novels. When my good wife would come in, I'd put my Bible on top of the story I was reading. But she knew what I was up to! I would try to excuse myself by saying that we couldn't always be reading the Scripture, that we needed a little variation.

I remember a prayer meeting. As we were in prayer, the Lord spoke to me. It was so audible that I opened my eyes and looked around. The voice said, "Pastor Tucker, ask your church to pray for you that you will have victory over your novels."

I argued, "What will these people think? They will lose confidence in me!"

But when the last person had finished praying, I said that I had a prayer request to make. "While you folks were praying, the Lord was talking to me about one of my weaknesses. He asked me to ask you people to pray that I will have victory over reading novels."

Well, they did—and it worked! I haven't read a novel since that day.

Sometimes, as his son, I am asked about my earliest recollections of my father's years in Montana. The thing I remember most clearly is Daddy's working in the garden. Regardless of where we lived, he always managed to grow things, perhaps deriving a certain strength from the soil. Even today, it is his practice to spend time working in the garden outside our headquarters, and he does this as often as possible.

Daddy was, of course, raising more than fruits and vegetables. Everywhere he ministered, in such places as Butte, Ronan, and Anaconda, he would raise up churches. He also made it a practice to assist those congregations in getting their own buildings. "If you leave a congregation in rented quarters, you don't know whether they are going to hold together or not," Daddy wisely observed. "But when you get a home for them, that's a real accomplishment."

His years of accomplishment in Montana led to a call to minister in another state, Colorado. At Craig, my father found only two Adventist families. But that was sufficient to begin evangelistic tent meetings and, eventually, to raise up a church.

As a boy of four, I discovered that my daddy could also raise something altogether unpleasant to me, if the need required. It was my job to gather eggs from the hay mow in the barn on our property. One day, when making my rounds, I observed my father coming down the ladder with eggs already collected in his hand.

"You darn fool—that's my job!" I informed him.

Daddy didn't like that kind of language. So he took me down to the harness room and said, "Sonny, you are going to have to be punished. I know you've heard some of the neighbor children use those words, but we just don't allow that kind of talk around here."

He left to take a strap off the harness, and I could envision great big welts about to rise on my bottom. After about five minutes (although it seemed like thirty to me), he returned, ready for action.

"Now, Son," he said, "before we have this spanking, we are going to kneel down and ask Jesus to forgive us."

"Daddy, I'll never do it again. So let's just pray about it—and that's all," I pleaded. I thought "let's just pray about it" was a good expression, and I repeated it from time to time, whenever I got into trouble.

But on this occasion, Daddy thought more than prayer was required. Taking that little piece of harness, he hit me three times.

Throughout the years, my father always reserved any discipline that may have been necessary for the proper time and place. It never occurred at the supper table, for instance, as it does today in many homes. Mother always tried to make the supper hour very cheerful. This was a time for happiness and for fellowship, not for scolding. Father was always of the same spirit, eternally optimistic. He usually came in with a song in his heart, radiating an inward happiness.

Years later when I was a teen-ager, if I would come in late, Daddy would confront me about it diplomatically. "Now, Son, you have disobeyed again. We told you to be in by ten o'clock, and here it is eleven. We have to have this stopped."

But the next morning, no matter what had taken place the night before, he would greet me enthusiastically. "It's a great day to be alive! Come on, Son. It's a beautiful day. Get up and at it!"

The beauty faded one day when Mother, who had often been sick with asthma, became critically ill. Everyone knew she was going to die. The entire church family filed silently by her bed, as Daddy stood at the head. Friends took us children off to other homes so that we wouldn't witness her final hours. But through the prayers of her husband and the church members, God reached down and touched Mother's body so that she recovered. Humanly speaking, I am not sure that Daddy could have recovered from Mother's death because of his great love for her.

Father was a kisser. He loved to kiss, and he taught us kids to do it, too. When we had family worship, we never finished without each one kissing the other. Mother and Daddy have always been very affectionate. In their tent home, when they were first married, they had a single rocking chair. He and Mother would both sit in it, she on his lap.

When we were living in Colorado, we had a big chair. I can remember Daddy's taking Mother (she was quite small, about a hundred pounds) and putting her on his lap. They would kiss and love each other this way after supper on many evenings.

Mother returned Daddy's affection in part because she hadn't received any from her father as she was growing up. I have heard my dear mother cry and say, "I was never kissed by my father, and my father said he was never kissed by his father." But in our home, love and kisses were the order of the day.

That's how Daddy is.

7

A Family Fashioned by Love

Daddy taught other important lessons to his young son, such as the necessity of doing one's best no matter what the task at hand. One day, I was half-heartedly hoeing the corn when he noticed my fooling around and my attempts to evade the job. He came out to see me about it.

"Son, I want to show you something. We are going to leave these four stalks you have just hoed just the way you left them. But the rest we are going to hoe the way they need to be cultivated, down around the roots.

"Let's see what happens as time passes. At first, you won't notice much difference. But in a month or so, you will see quite a contrast."

From time to time that summer, he would take me out to make an inspection. The four stalks I had treated so indifferently turned out to be poor, weakly things that didn't reach more than three feet in height. But the corn stalks that had been properly hoed grew to more than six feet and produced luscious ears. I got the lesson.

Daddy took time from his busy schedule to teach me how to plow straight. "You see that stake at the end of the row? Keep your eyes on it as you plow. Don't look to the right; don't look to the left. Just go straight ahead." I learned how to set a goal and to pursue it directly.

After a few years, the Tucker family moved from Craig to Delta, Colorado, to pastor a church there. After getting nicely settled, Daddy was asked to preach in Farmington, New Mexico, a part of the Inter-Mountain Conference. In this community, Daddy had an experience he loves to relate.

While holding nightly meetings, Daddy observed a group of high school young people who showed up for each service. Among them was a girl named Helen, who lived alone with her widowed father, keeping house for him.

"Where are you going every night?" he asked his daughter.

"Down to hear that young preacher at the Adventist church."

"Well, I'd rather have you go to meetings than to be chasing about on the streets. But don't you get interested in all those Adventists. Remember that I kicked your brother out of the house for joining the Presbyterians."

But the young girl did get interested. And when it came time for a baptismal class to be formed, she said she wanted to join it. My daddy reminded the young girl of the threat her father had made.

"But this means everything to me—more than life itself," she pleaded.

Daddy suggested that she tell that to her father and wait until another baptismal service the following Sabbath. She complied.

"Just remember what I told you," her father stormed. "We can't have any other religions than my religion in this home. If you insist on going ahead with those Adventists, you'll have to leave as soon as school is out."

The young lady went ahead and was baptized by my daddy, as she had wished. As it turned out, she didn't have to leave home. She lived her new faith before her father. Eventually, she went away to an Adventist college, married a preacher, and became a worker for God.

My father is fond of relating this incident to show the importance of standing up for one's commitment, even if it means the risk of losing home and family.

Family life, in the Tucker household was, of course, entirely different, especially as it concerned preparation for Sabbath observance. Friday would be a busy day as we children shined shoes, helped clean the house, trimmed the grass, and took baths. About a half hour before sundown, mother would gather the family around the piano and start playing the hymn, "Day Is Dying in the West." Then we would sing other familiar hymns. This marked the beginning of sundown worship. Each week, favorite Bible verses were repeated from memory.

Daddy would sit in his big chair, open his Bible, and read to the family. Fascinating stories of Bible heroes like David, Daniel and Elijah kept us children on the edge of our chairs. We always closed family worship with everyone taking time to pray.

Friday night supper was always special. Mother would prepare some delightful dessert, such as cinnamon rolls. The aroma of freshly baked bread would bring the family to the table. Often Daddy would have a Friday night meeting somewhere; and on these occasions, we children were permitted to attend.

Since youth, my father had practiced getting up at 5:30 or 6:00 on Sabbath mornings and on weekday mornings as well. And I would get up with him on Sabbaths, and sometimes we would eat breakfast together. Mother preferred to stay up late in the evenings and to sleep late in the mornings.

We would go to Sabbath school as a family and then to church. Often we would bring home guests for lunch, if Mother felt up to it. Sometimes we would take a picnic lunch to a remote place in the hills or down by the river or lake or out in some field under the trees. We could hardly wait until dinner was over for the long walk with Daddy through nature to get better acquainted with God's creation.

On the way home, almost invariably, there would be some sick or shut-in person to visit. Father would say, "Now, I want you children to sing for Mrs. Jones," and we did. We absorbed from our parents the philosophy of helping to bring comfort and cheer to people.

The day would close with sundown worship and

immediately plans would be formulated as to how to observe the next Sabbath in some special way.

The family drew even closer, if that were possible, when we moved from the center of town to a home two miles north. An acre of ground was devoted to a garden and orchard. Daddy taught me how to plant, weed, and harvest.

Yet, he mixed work with play. Our home had originally been a community center of thirteen rooms. One of these we turned into a handball court. When Daddy was able to spend a few days at home between evangelistic meetings, we would play handball every day.

That quality family time that Daddy valued so highly continued even after he left Colorado to serve the Adventist Church of St. Paul, Minnesota. This was the first time we had lived in a big city, and Daddy didn't like it. As soon as he could, he moved us so that we could spend summers on a lake.

One of the first things Father did was to buy some horseshoes and drive spikes at the required distances. "I'm going to be gone for a while, Son" he told me, "but I want you to practice hard so that you can beat me when I return."

"Okay, Daddy, I'll beat you!"

When he returned, he beat me soundly, as might be expected. But I would challenge him every time he came home from meetings.

The church itself in St. Paul provided a different kind of challenge. The ninety-nine members of the congregation met in a beautiful Baptist church and were quite content to continue their rental arrangement indefinitely. The conference president told the newly arrived pastor, "Your church needs its own building."

"But the leaders are happy with things as they are," Father answered. "How can I get them to build?"

"I don't know, but find a way."

Father went directly to the pastor of the Baptist church and asked him pointedly, "Do you love us?"

"Why, yes, certainly."

"Do you love us enough to put us out?" Daddy explained that so long as his people were comfortable renting the big, beautiful church, they wouldn't budge. "Make up some excuse and put us out."

The Baptist minister decided on the spot that the church suddenly needed redecorating and wrote Father a note saying that on a certain date they would have to terminate their friendly relationship.

On their final Sabbath in the church, the conference president spoke, reminding the congregation of how Jacob labored seven years for Rachel and got Leah instead. "You folks have been here seven years, and you don't even have your Leah!"

Daddy's flock rented an old dance hall that reeked of cigarette smoke and alcohol. That fired the congregation to action. Soon they were able to buy a beautiful stone church and renovate it to meet their growing needs. Daddy considers this one of the highlights of his stay in St. Paul.

But Father's ministry in Minnesota was by no means confined to St. Paul, as I have suggested. He traveled frequently to other parts of the state to hold evangelistic services, even during what were supposed to be vacations. At Red Wing, he conducted an open-air meeting in a secluded part of the city. A group responded to the messages and organized a church.

An extended summertime outreach took place in Rochester, Minnesota. Daddy was instrumental in raising up a small congregation; later a church was built. At the dedication service, attended by the conference president and the union president, the mayor of Rochester welcomed Father to the city and then fell over dead, stricken by a sudden heart attack. That unexpected event cast a somber note over what was to have been a joyous occasion, but it pointedly illustrated the brevity of life and the need to be right with God.

Father saw the great need for people to be right with each other. At this same Rochester tabernacle, Pastor Tucker was asked by a middle-aged lady at the close of a service if he would perform a wedding ceremony for her. This was her strange story:

Thirty-six years ago, I married a wonderful man who was a wealthy farmer. He had two farms that joined each other. We were radiantly happy for three years until we had a violent quarrel and got a divorce. I took one farm and he the other.

I never looked at another man for thirty-three years, and he never looked at another woman for thirty-three years. We were both stubborn. He would not come to me, and I would not go to him to seek reconciliation, though my pillow was often wet with tears. Finally, after all this time, he contracted a terrible illness and was rushed to the hospital. He hovered between life and death.

I couldn't stay away. I had to go. At the hospital, the

people wouldn't let me in because they thought it might be too great an emotional stress on him. But I watched, and when nobody was around, I slipped into his room, and there he was, eyes closed. I walked up to his bed, leaned over and kissed him on the mouth.

He didn't open his eyes, but he said, "You still love me, don't you."

I told him that I had always loved him and had always waited for him these thirty-three years.

That's my story, Pastor Tucker. He wants to marry me again. I wonder if you would perform the ceremony.

Father said he would be delighted. The next day, she came into the meeting place, bringing her former husband in a wheelchair. Father helped the man to his feet and reunited them in marriage. Whenever he tells this story, he stresses how stubbornness can ruin a lifetime of happiness and how Jesus condemned straining at gnats and swallowing camels.

My father's service in Minnesota, effective though it was, came to a conclusion in its fifth year. The Lord was about to take him to another city where he would begin an outreach that would, in time, touch all parts of the world for Christ.

8

The Quiet Hour

A busy pastor needs a vacation from time to time, and so my father decided to take the train from St. Paul to visit his parents who were now living in California. He passed through Oregon on the way. While the trip was in progress, Daddy noticed a fellow traveler reading his Bible, with an Adventist church paper and yearbook close at hand.

Father moved over to introduce himself. "I'm Pastor Tucker. I'm glad to see you are reading the Good Book. I assume that you are an Adventist."

The man smiled and identified himself as Pastor N. C. Wilson, president of the Southeast Asia Union Mission. He invited the young minister to have dinner with him and to share the journey. As it turned out, this man was to speak in the Portland area. A large group turned out at the station to meet him, and my daddy was standing by his side. The folks were introduced to the St. Paul pastor; and before long, they extended an invitation to him to minister on the West Coast. The year was 1935.

The old Central Adventist Church had been the pioneer congregation of the Portland area and had mothered seven other churches. Father considers his eight years in Portland as pastor of this church and later of the Tabernacle Church of the same city as among the most happy and productive of his life. This period turned out to be the turning point of his ministry.

Two outstanding Adventist evangelists, Melvin and Dan Venden, came to Portland and preached to large crowds in a tabernacle. To advertise their outreach, they contracted with radio station KEX, a fifty-thousand-watt outlet, for three half-hour broadcasts weekly. Before the one-year contract was completed, the Venden brothers accepted an invitation to hold meetings in the East. They recommended to the conference president that my father be chosen to complete the contract on KEX. "His voice and personality will be good," they said.

Later, the conference president came to my father and said, "Pastor Tucker, would you like to assume this broadcasting responsibility and take over the time on KEX?"

This offer came as a shock. My father had never entertained any dreams or plans of being a radio preacher. But now he laid the matter before the Lord to seek His direction. At last, he formulated a reply. "If the conference brethren will allow me to go down to Glendale to consult with H.M.S. Richards, I will consider the matter."

Father chose a good model. There was no finer broadcast minister than Richards of *The Voice of*

Prophecy, then a weekly radio broadcast on the West Coast, which later became known internationally for its quality and effectiveness.

For three days, my father talked with this highly respected broadcaster and observed the operation and organization of his radio program. They tested father's potential and made a sample broadcast. That fine, rich bass voice which my father had once used to sing to the cows on a South Dakota farm proved to be perfectly molded for use on the airwaves. H.M.S. Richards encouraged my father to go ahead and begin broadcasting. Back home again in Portland, he told the conference president of his decision: "I'll do my best to make the broadcast a soul-winning agency, but I'll need your prayers and your support."

Father had always been nervous before speaking to church audiences. This is one reason why he developed his humor, a trait for which he is known. He used it to break the ice, to warm up the audience, and to set himself more at ease.

But what would it be like to talk over the air to an unseen audience that might be critical of their untried speaker? The very thought terrified him. Finally, the day of the first broadcast came, July 7, 1937. A few minutes before air time, Father went to the studio, in his words, "scared stiff."

He was. I was there as a fifteen-year-old boy, and I remember the occasion very well. Daddy sat at a table with a microphone before him. He had his Bible in his hands, but they were shaking so hard he had to lay it down. Then he would nervously pick it up again, only to put it down once more. His knees were knocking so much that they hit against the table and moved it. At the proper moment, the announcer "threw the cue" and this first broadcast of *The Quiet Hour* was underway.

The beautiful voice of Harold Graham, who called himself the "West Coast Gospel Singer," sounded forth, accompanied by Elsie Fitzgerald, the organist. Father had almost memorized his sermon, and somehow got through it. A sigh of relief went up from all of us when the red light went off, signifying that the broadcast had been completed.

Right from the very first broadcast there was an excellent mail response. Although *The Quiet Hour* was officially announced as being conference-sponsored, the twelve-dollar-a-week broadcast was paid for by listeners who appreciated the ministry and who wished to support it. In fact, the financial response was so good that soon the broadcast became a daily ministry, then a twice-daily ministry, fourteen broadcasts a week. In those early days, there was no tape recording equipment or direct lines into the church to enable broadcasts to be made from the sanctuary. So fourteen times a week, Father and his musicians made their way to the radio studio to do their broadcasts "live."

Later, *The Quiet Hour* sponsored a dramatic program called *The Friendly Neighbors*, modeled after a secular broadcast entitled *The Seth Parker Program*. The neighbors would come together to sing and talk over problems and events in their lives and in the world. They always found the answer to their problems from the Bible, which Uncle Jim (Pastor Tucker) gave. It was my privilege, as my father's young son, to have a part in this series.

Daddy has always enjoyed tremendous physical energy. But even he found the fast pace as a broadcaster and pastor taxing. Eventually, he developed bleeding ulcers, and the doctor advised an operation.

"I thought that was inconsistent," Daddy recalls. "Here I was praying for other people that they'd get well, and here I was about to go into the hospital." After delaying the procedure as long as he could and praying a Pauline prayer that this thorn in the flesh might be taken away, he had one third of his stomach removed by the surgeon.

The daily radio broadcasts, of course, had to continue. But who would be the speaker? My mother stepped into the gap and did the programs for the next three weeks. Was she frightened of this assignment?

"I may have been," Mother remembers, "because I was generally scared of anything I did. But it didn't worry me. I just went in there and did it!"

The Lord speeded Daddy's recovery, and he has enjoyed remarkably good health over his long and vigorous life.

Doing fourteen broadcasts each week required a considerable amount of time in preparation. Daddy didn't hesitate to borrow material that was better than he thought he could produce himself. Once this got him into some friendly trouble.

"I stole some stuff from Brother Varner Johns, an old friend of mine. He had been my conference president in Minnesota. He was living in San Diego, and my late night broadcast from Portland carried that far. He turned on his radio one night; and after listening for a while, he said to his wife, 'That Tucker fellow has got something that's good.' Later he said to her, 'That sounds familiar.' And then it dawned on him—'I wrote that!' "

According to Daddy, the only redeeming feature of his stealing material was that he always stole good stuff. His San Diego friend was most gracious and shared in the laugh. After that, Daddy was scrupulous in giving credit when he used someone else's material.

Later, my father began to write books and booklets for giving away on broadcasts. One literature thrust began with the very first year of broadcasting, and it has become one of the most important ministries of *The Quiet Hour*. I refer to the monthly paper God has so widely used, *The Quiet Hour Echoes*. This little publication, filled with news of the broadcasts, missions' outreach, sermons, poems, and gems of thought, both informs and inspires.

If you had been a subscriber back in July, 1942, you would have probably read the lead article, which in part reads as follows:

The Quiet Hour Completes
Five Years of Service

Five years! How quickly they have gone! What opportunities they have presented. Eternity alone will reveal the full fruitage of this most modern method of sowing the Gospel seed. It has been a joy to conduct THE QUIET HOUR Radio Program each day. Quietly the seeds of truth have been started, interest in spiritual things has been created.

The Quiet Hour

How our hearts have thrilled as word has come in of discouraged souls who were in the very act of destroying their own lives, who for some unexplained reason have turned on their radio and heard words of life and hope. Many have been the bedridden, dying ones who found light and courage as they went down into the valley of deep shadows.

Many scornful doubters have listened to a sound basis for faith and have been led to cry like Thomas, "My Lord and my God." Clouds of prejudice and misconception that have filled the mind of thousands concerning God's message for this hour have unconsciously receded and disappeared before the blessing of God's grace as it has rested upon THE QUIET HOUR ministry in song and word.

The grace of God, which had proved so adequate in Portland, would soon be demonstrated to the Tuckers in a new field of service.

9

Knocking
at the Golden Gate

The radio signal that reached as far south as San Diego and the California-Mexico border also boomed, of course, right into the San Francisco Bay area. Over a period of time, my father became increasingly known on the West Coast. Eventually, the Northern California Conference called Father to be the pastor of the six-hundred-member Berkeley Adventist Church.

Leaving Portland after a fruitful ministry of eight years proved difficult. Daddy wrote in *The Quiet Hour Echoes* of November, 1943,

Goodbyes are hard to say. Yet, in the life of a minister the call to Abraham is often repeated. The years we have spent in Portland have been happy, busy ones. God has been good to us. Despite human frailties, there has been much fruitage as a result of the daily radio programs, coupled with the Tabernacle meetings. To every soul who has in any way contributed to the joy of our ministry here, we take this means of saying, again, thank you and God bless you!

When Father moved south, everything pertaining

to the radio ministry except the name *The Quiet Hour* was left behind, including office furniture and mailing lists of thousands of names. But he immediately pushed plans to establish a daily radio program in the populous Bay area.

World War II was still on when my father and his family moved to Berkeley in 1943. Since it was impossible to get priorities for lumber to build churches or schools, there was ample money for broadcasting. "Don't spare the horses," the conference brethren told him. "Just buy all the time you want. And don't ask for listeners to support you."

This last statement conflicted with a philosophy my father had developed from his first days on the air. "I would prefer that a hundred people give me a dollar a week than have one person give me a hundred dollars," he explained. "That way I have more folks praying for me."

The brethren didn't think the concept of listener support would work, based on their past experiences. But they were willing to let Father do it his way.

Father contracted to buy time on a small, five-hundred-watt station, KRE. The daily broadcasts on that outlet began to attract a growing audience. Before long, it was possible to add a second, larger station, KROW in Oakland. That radio outreach was also well-received.

A broadcast ministry consists of far more than sitting before a microphone and talking. The program itself is merely the tip of the iceberg. Broadcasting is long hours of preparation, staffing, making technical arrangements, receiving and answering letters, record-keeping, making bank deposits, paying bills, compiling mailing lists, and much more. Those thousands of listeners who were tuning in each day to one or more of father's radio broadcasts probably had no idea of the organization or complexity involved. But Daddy did, and he set out to solve the problem.

In downtown Oakland at 1320 Webster Street, *The Quiet Hour* leased a vacant two-story building and remodeled it to meet its growing and varied needs. The broadcast studio had glass panels in the wall so that visitors could come in and watch the programs being aired. A chapel seated 150 people. There was a bookstore—where people could buy religious literature, Bibles, and records—and a private reading room. A prayer room offered visitors opportunity to pray for their needs, alone or with members of the staff. And those who needed spiritual advice could receive it in the counseling room. The secretarial offices were located in the rear of the building where many details essential to keeping *The Quiet Hour* ministry going efficiently and effectively were cared for. In all, the Oakland headquarters proved to be a great step in advancing the Lord's work from 1945 to 1954.

Daddy never considered himself a good ad-libber before the microphone. So he made it a practice to write out in longhand all of his radio talks in advance. "I work better behind a pencil," he would say. This solid preparation helped to take away some of his natural shyness and nervousness.

What might have seemed to be a handicap actually turned out to be a great asset. At the start of his radio ministry, Father began buying little booklets to offer over the air as encouragement for listeners to write and support the programs. As the years passed, Father was building up a tremendous amount of excellent material that he had written. Gradually, he began making available booklets that bore his own by-line and concentrated on material he had researched and knew best.

For example, Father had long been an admirer of Abraham Lincoln and had perhaps a dozen books on this great American in his library. So as the anniversary of Lincoln's birthday approached, Father wrote a pamphlet and made it available. The response was good. Soon there appeared booklets to honor mother on Mother's Day, father on Father's Day, etc. It proved to be less expensive to write and produce his own materials than it was to buy what someone else had written. Listeners appreciated the literature supplement, and this aspect of *The Quiet Hour* began to grow rapidly.

Father writes in what he calls "Tucker language." By that, he means he phrases his writing in a simple way so that people can readily understand it. He never attempts to be eloquent, but just to speak to a mythical "Aunt Sue" sitting alone in a farmhouse in Iowa. "I just come in for a visit with her."

In addition to his writing ministry, my father was also continuing to publish *The Quiet Hour Echoes*, as he had done from the very first. This monthly publication, which has now expanded to sixteen pages, has always carried news of the broadcast, plus much inspiration and blessing independent of the radio outreach. It may come as a surprise to learn that thousands of people who subscribe to *The Echoes* never hear a broadcast, because the program is not released in their areas. But they enjoy what this little paper adds to their homes and lives and have become faithful supporters.

Reaching people has always been my father's objective, whether in a personal pastoral outreach or through broadcasting. But one man, even one with tremendous physical and spiritual energy, can accomplish only so much by himself. When asked to become the pastor of the Grand Avenue Church of Oakland, Father agreed on one condition, that he have an ordained minister as an associate. The conference president asked, "Who do you have in mind?" Without a moment's hesitation, Father replied, "It has always been a dream of mine to have my son work with me. He has recently been ordained and would be my choice."

From childhood, I had always wanted to be a preacher, possibly because Daddy was a preacher. Father had a black bag that he would take with him on preaching missions. I remember grabbing it one day as a lad of six or seven, heading for the door and announcing, "I gotta go preach like Daddy."

I recall Mother in her prayer room crying out loud to God on my behalf. "Oh, God, we dedicated La Verne to You before he was ever born. He is to be a worker for You. Oh, God, help us to know how to train him."

When I was eight years old, a missionary by the name of Davies came to our church to speak. When the service was over, he shook hands with the folks at the door. And without knowing who I was, he said to me,

"Little fellow, what do you want to be when you grow up?"

"I don't know," I replied. "Maybe a cowboy."

"Well, I'm sure God has some big plans for you, Son. I tell you what. You go home and think it over, and then come back and tell me about it after the story hour."

When my father brought Mr. Davies home for lunch, I was embarrassed for fear that he might recognize me and ask his question as to my future before the whole family.

I received permission to be excused from the table, even before dessert was served, something highly unusual for me, and went off to my room to consider the matter. I plopped on my bed and thought about what I might possibly be when I grew up. The image of a football player came to mind, then a baseball catcher. But nothing seemed appealing.

Finally, after about an hour, I got down on my knees and said, "Dear Jesus, I don't know what I am supposed to be, but whatever You want me to be, that's what I want to be." Though not by an audible voice, at that moment the Lord gave me a clear message as to His desires for my life. I jumped up and said confidently, "Now I know what I am going to be!"

In a few minutes Father announced that it was time to go to meeting. I knew what I was going to be when I grew up, so I wasn't afraid to see that fellow Davies again. Sure enough, after the stories were over, the missionary went to the door to shake hands with the people as they left. When I came by he said, "Aren't you the little fellow that I asked this morning about what you were going to be?"

I drew myself up to my full three feet and announced, "I'm going to be a missionary like you and a preacher like my daddy!" So from the age of eight, I had no doubt as to what work God had called me to perform.

After graduating from Portland Union Academy, I went off to Walla Walla College in Washington to study for the ministry. During my senior year, my wife and I teamed with another couple to hold evangelistic meetings in Waitsburg, Washington. I took courses in broadcasting and conducted two program series over a Walla Walla station. I came out of school determined to use radio as an evangelistic tool.

After four months of evangelism in Polson, Montana, my first pastorate was right back in the place where I had lived as a boy—the Butte-Helena-Anaconda district. After three years, we were called to the Payette district where continual evangelistic meetings were held in Vale and Nissa, Oregon, and New Plymouth and Payette, Idaho.

I was ordained to the ministry in my fourth year, and the following year was called to work by my father's side in the Grand Avenue Church in Oakland. My father's wish and dream that we should one day work together had come true.

In the spring of 1949, representatives of powerful radio station KGO contacted my father and informed him that the station was expanding into television. The station had chosen *The Quiet Hour* to be "simulcast" on their station—both radio and television released at the same time—at 7:30 on Saturday nights.

Immediately, my father responded, "Oh, no! Television is too frightening. We could do the radio part, but not television. After all, who would want to look at this homely face?"

The idea of going on television was dropped, but the sales manager contacted my father about a wonderful opening on KGO radio. Readers of the *Echoes* received an extra-special edition outlining the good news. The headline read: "A Great Opportunity and a Mighty Challenge." Here, in part, is the story:

Radio station KGO, a fifty-thousand-watt station in San Francisco, has changed its policy and will now accept a few choice religious programs. They have honored us by giving us first chance among the local broadcasters to purchase time. Tentatively they will hold open for us one half-hour, five nights a week, immediately following the popular Richfield news broadcast, which has an audience of 1,250,000 listeners. KGO covers an immense area from Canada to Mexico and far to the east. We feel it is a divine opening and that we ought to go forward.

So did the listeners. Soon *The Quiet Hour* staff (my father, the quartet, and an organist) were making the nightly trip from Oakland to the studies of KGO in uptown San Francisco to broadcast another *Quiet Hour* program. This made four daily broadcasts, twenty-eight broadcasts a week: 7:30 A.M. and 1:30 P.M. on station KRE, 7:30 P.M. on KROW, and 10:15 P.M. on KGO. This was just too much; so after two months of exhaustion, the station offered us an early morning time slot at 6:00 A.M. daily. Except for the months of May, June, and July, this hour had by far the greatest response of all our broadcasts. Tape recording had been developed by then, and the station would accept a high-quality production. Therefore, our 7:30 P.M. KROW program was taped and sent to KGO each day.

Think of that demanding schedule! Fortunately, Daddy didn't have to appear at each station in person. Instead, Class–A telephone lines were connected from *The Quiet Hour* studio directly to the stations involved. Just at air time, a red light would flash on, indicating that the program was on the air.

"Tucker, you're working too hard," one conference official told the busy radio pastor. "Take it easy. Take a vacation."

Father answered, "My brother, Sister White would turn over in her grave if she ever heard you advising a worker to slack off and ease up."*

"But one denominational broadcast a week ought to be enough," the official countered.

Daddy had a quick answer: "Is that the way the liquor and tobacco folks do? Do they just have one announcement once a week? Why, they pound it into the listeners day after day, several times a day." To make sure of his facts, Father called a station to find out just how much time was devoted to selling alcohol and cigarettes. When the church official heard the total, he had to back off from his criticism.

The bottom line in broadcasting, of course, centers

---

*Sister White was one of the founders of the Seventh-day Adventist denomination.

on the effects that the programs have on listeners. Are they moved, awakened to their spiritual needs, changed? These are the basic issues. Father has many illustrations that indicate how God has used *The Quiet Hour* over the years. The following is one of his favorites.

Daddy was giving a series of Bible messages on his weeknight broadcasts. He talked on "Why I Believe the Bible," and he followed this with "Why I Believe in the God of the Bible." In each series he listed specific logical reasons for his Christian faith. Then he turned to the Person of Christ in a series entitled "Why I Believe in the Divinity of Christ" and another, "Why I Believe Jesus is the Messiah."

Unknown to him, two elderly brothers sat listening in a hotel room. When Father had completed his series of "Why I Believe," one of them made his way to the studio and asked to see Pastor Tucker. He was shown in. The moment he met Daddy, tears filled his eyes; he said, "You will never know the joy that has come into our lives because of your broadcasts."

Father had a pressing speaking engagement some distance away, so he responded, "I am busy, but let's hear the high points of your story." How close Daddy had come to missing a memorable experience that has encouraged him so many times!

The elderly man revealed that when he was a boy, evangelist J. N. Loughborough had come to his town to hold public meetings. Although his family thought the evangelist was preaching heresy, his father had decided to go to the meetings in order to "protect the community from false doctrines." His father was a well-respected lawyer, priding himself in always being on the right side of every issue and refusing ever to be a party to anything that would compromise the truth.

People in town breathed easier when they learned the lawyer would be at the meetings. For the first few nights, nothing controversial was discussed. Then the topic turned to why people ought to keep the Sabbath. At this point the lawyer stood up and openly challenged the evangelist to allow him to take the pulpit and show the community "the real truth of the matter."

Graciously, the evangelist agreed, declaring that above all else he wanted the truth of God's Word presented. The lawyer requested two days' time to prepare, and there was no small speculation on how the lawyer would show up the preacher.

When the appointed time came, the tent was filled to overflowing. The lawyer was the first to speak, and here is what he said:

Ladies and gentlemen, I have lived in this community for a long time and have conducted myself in such a way as to command the respect of the good people of this area. You know how it has always been my policy to be on the right side of every question, whether it's been popular or unpopular. I have never knowingly tried to defend or uphold a lie or tried to make black look white. I have studied long hours the subject of the seventh day Sabbath that the preacher told us about, which I sincerely thought was heresy, but I find that he is on the right side of this question; and with his permission I would like to follow my rule of life and join him and get on the right side of this Sabbath truth.

It created a sensation! Many townspeople followed the lawyer in baptism.

My father's visitor continued to reveal that as a result of this, the family's members were all raised in the church, except his oldest brother who had said he could not believe in the God of the Bible. Their parents earnestly prayed that the entire family would be together on Resurrection morning. However, after the passage of a great many years, both brothers ended up in a backslidden condition. In the winter they shared an apartment in the city, and together they would listen to Pastor Tucker's broadcast in the evening. Pastor Tucker seemed to be speaking directly to them.

One night at the close of the broadcast, the elder brother, now in his nineties, turned to his companion and said, "I can now believe in the God of the Bible. Oh, why could I not see it before!" He scolded his younger brother severely for having abandoned his original position of faith, and they knelt together by their radio, poured out their confession of the wrongs of so many years, and called on divine grace.

Father is still moved whenever he relates this incident. He says:

God, let me be a part of that answer for all those years of prayers on this old man's behalf. Those petitions finally got through to the throne of God, and He let me bring the answer to them.

I think this should be a great encouragement to mothers and fathers who simply and earnestly pray for the salvation of their children. God will turn heaven and earth upside down to answer. He may even use a farmer boy like me to do it.

Yes, radio did bring results.

10
Start and Keep Going

As Father's broadcasting ministry expanded, so did his pastoral duties. Many of those who listened to him on the air each day had no church home. So often when a family member became sick or injured, the parent or spouse would call up and ask Pastor Tucker to visit him or her in the hospital. If there was a death, he was asked to officiate at the funeral.

One such experience involved a little girl named Bonnie. Its similarity to an incident in the healing ministry of our Lord is amazing. But let Father tell the story.

> A lady called me from a hospital in San Francisco. "Pastor Tucker, they tell me my little Bonnie is dying and that there is no hope. Won't you come and pray? I know that God can do anything and everything."
>
> The dear lady went on to tell how her little one had been born with a defective heart; as she was growing older, her heart condition worsened. A

heart specialist, after an examination, told the mother there was a fifty-fifty chance a delicate heart operation would help. Without it, the child would live only a few months. The surgery was performed and was at first thought to be successful, but then Bonnie went into convulsions.

The doctor told her mother, "Prepare your heart for the worst. She cannot live. There has never been a case in medical history where this delicate operation has been performed upon a person who developed these reactions and lived."

But the mother had faith. She told her physician, "But my Bonnie can live. God can hear and answer. May I call my pastor?" The man agreed, thinking that a minister could at least provide some comfort. I drove over to Mount Zion Hospital. As I was going up the steps, another minister met me there, for the mother had called him also.

We went into the room where the little one was with her mother, the nurse, and the doctor. There was no time for talking, so we knelt down and offered an earnest prayer. Then I anointed Bonnie with oil, as the Bible tells us to do. After finishing the prayer, I said, "Bonnie, in the name of Jesus, be made whole."

When we arose to our feet, the little one had gone to sleep, I thought. But the doctor said she had lapsed into a coma and would not waken. But just then the little girl opened her eyes, and she saw me, a total stranger. She looked a little scared. Then she saw her mother and smiled. She said, "Momma, I'm hungry."

Her mother looked at the doctor, and he nodded his head. "Bonnie," her mother asked, "what do you want?" Bonnie asked for ice cream. The doctor went out into the hall, put a dime in a machine, and came back with an ice cream bar, which the little girl ate.

Jesus had heard the heart-cry of that mother, had seen her faith, and had healed her daughter. She spoke of Bonnie as her miracle baby.

The doctor said to me, "I never believed in miracles before, but I do now!" And when the dear mother went to the heart specialist to thank him for his wonderful work, he stopped her, pointed to the skies, and replied, "God did this one." Bonnie is now a grown woman.

Father considers this one of the sweetest experiences of his life, and he is fond of relating the story.

People also called my father when they fell in love. The problem of an officiating minister for a marriage had to be decided. "Why not Brother Tucker of *The Quiet Hour*?" Daddy would soon have another appointment to add to his crowded schedule. Over the years, he performed thousands of weddings and conducted many funerals.

To those who asked how one man could accomplish so much, Father would relate the story of how he had come across a little boy chinning himself on a bar.

"How many times can you go up and down like that?" he asked the lad.

"Oh, forty or fifty times."

Daddy asked if he could try it. He managed exactly one chin-up.

"The secret," the boy said encouragingly, "is to start and to keep going!" And with that, the little fellow began chinning himself again.

Father learned a lesson from this incident—that having begun well, all that he had to do was to continue. "If you love a thing, you get tired, yes, but you are just as eager to come back again every morning and get with it again."

Even today, when he goes out to speak, Father recommends the same rigorous schedule to younger pastors. And he also urges them to see the possibilities of beginning a radio ministry on their own. "If you want your work to grow and expand," he tells them, "get on the air every day for fifteen minutes or at least five. That's the way to reach people."

Our good friend, George Vandeman, came from Washington, D.C., where he was serving as one of the leaders of the ministerial association of our church. He encouraged us to go on television with our *Quiet Hour* format. Four months later, he returned and asked if we had investigated the cost. Finally, he insisted that we find out.

I went to the telephone and called KGO-TV and was told, "If you sign a contract today, a half hour will cost only one hundred dollars per telecast, but if signed tomorrow, the half hour at 7:30 Saturday night will cost two hundred dollars."

When I told Pastor Vandeman this news, he said, "Let's drive over and see their set-up." Father was hesitant, but he finally agreed to go. After seeing the modest facilities, we went into a small room and prayed together for guidance. After prayer, it was decided that we should sign the one-year contract to go on KGO-TV at 7:30 each Saturday night.

Our first telecast was on November 23, 1949. At that time, there were only 17,000 TV sets in the entire Bay area. One year later, there were more than 350,000 sets in use. So we were certainly pioneers, not only for the industry but also for our church, as there was no regular, weekly television ministry of our church in the country. What a challenge—fifty-two consecutive, live Saturday night programs!

The general format of *The Quiet Hour* telecast was much the same as that of the radio broadcast. Music included the same quartet, using male quartet music. (My wife, Alma, sang first tenor, I sang bass, and two other men completed the group.) Besides preparing songs for two live radio broadcasts daily, my responsibility included writing the TV scripts, the Bible stories for children, and directing the program. My father and I took turns presenting the thirteen-minute, heart-to-heart messages.

Looking back on that year of pioneering in the field of television gospel ministry, we can see God's wonderful leading and blessing. But with the 1,456 radio broadcasts—730 of them live—providing two or three songs for each broadcast, conducting evangelistic crusades, and meeting public appearances weekly, the entire operation can best be described as "fast and furious."

Two things took place to end the television ministry

and our father/son working relationship, things which at first seemed impossible to understand but which, in retrospect, were obviously of the Lord.

First, on the local level the conference president felt it was not good to have a father and son ministerial team. Then, Daddy received a telephone call from Washington, D.C., asking him to give up his personal television ministry in favor of a denominational television outreach. Although very disappointed at receiving this request, he willingly cooperated and our television ministry was discontinued for a time.

I was asked to pastor a district of three churches with Redding, California, as our home. Daddy continued his radio broadcasting in Oakland for another few years. We didn't suspect then that God would soon put us together again to see strange things and faraway places.

11

An Enlarged Vision
of the World

In November, 1949, Adali Esteb was one of our guests on our early afternoon broadcast on KRE. Pastor Esteb had spent years as a missionary in Korea and at that time was director of our annual worldwide mission outreach. Father asked Pastor Esteb what a gift of one thousand dollars would accomplish in the mission field. Brother Esteb graphically described what a tremendous blessing that amount would bring to a certain mission field.

In the next day's mail came a check for $1,000 from a first-time writer, with a request that these funds be used as was described by Pastor Esteb. The letter bore a local address, so Father got in his car, intending to thank the woman contributor in person. When he was unable to gain admission to her home, he returned to the office and wrote a personal letter of appreciation.

The lady responded with an invitation to see her. She explained that she never saw anyone except by appointment because she was wealthy and constantly beseiged by people wanting help.

"I used to see heads of colleges and universities come in and talk to my parents and walk out with checks for thirty or forty thousand dollars in their pockets," she told him. "My folks were rich. We used to think, as kids, that they were going to give it all away, but they didn't."

The gracious lady extended to Father an invitation to come back and visit her each week. On one visit, Father incidentally mentioned that he was having to make three or four extra recordings daily to get enough ahead so he could be gone a month. He explained that Pastor H.M.S. Richards of *The Voice of Prophecy* broadcast had invited him to come along with him to the Holy Land.

"Oh," she said, "when you go there you should keep on going around the world visiting all those wonderful mission stations that you tell us about. And I'm going to see to it that you do just that. You need to bring back to us a firsthand report of the needs of these areas. Now, you make out a list of the places that you want to visit, and I'll take care of the air ticket. And not only for you, but also for Mrs. Tucker."

Father thanked her for her generous offer but explained that Mother was not strong and that the tour would be too strenuous for her. Then she suggested, "If Mrs. Tucker is unable to go with you, then I want your son, LaVerne, to go. I've appreciated his evangelistic meetings so much."

"I'm sure La Verne would be thrilled by this oppor-

Julius and Ida were wed on July 4, 1917.

The first broadcast of *The Quiet Hour* originated in Portland, Oregon, on July 7, 1937. L. to R.—Harold Graham, J. L. Tucker, Elsie Fitzgerald.

The Quiet Hour telecast on KGO-TV, San Francisco, ran for fifty-two consecutive Saturday nights in 1948. L. to R.—Jean Wallace, Preston Wallace, Alma Tucker (La Verne's wife), Richard Lange, L.E. Tucker, J.L. Tucker.

Today J. L. and son, L. E., share the ministry of *The Quiet Hour* at its headquarters in Redlands, California. The weekly radio broadcast is carried by more than 450 stations nationwide. The *Search* telecast has a growing influence, being televised by more than 60 stations.

Pastor Tucker, eighty-one, is still putting in a full day as director and principal speaker of *The Quiet Hour.*

Four generations of Tucker males (three of whom are ministers): Julius, LaVerne, Bill, and Chad.

Ida, J. L., L. E., and Alma Tucker, 1978.

tunity, and it would be a blessing to him throughout his ministry," responded my father.

"Fine. I'll pay his way and the remainder of your expenses as well!"

That's the way God provided the finances for Daddy and me to visit our mission stations around the world in 1953. H.M.S. Richards had to cancel his plans for the trip, but we decided to push on by ourselves. God was about to use another means to open up an opportunity that might otherwise have been closed to us.

Father received a letter from Elder Branson, at that time president of the denomination's general conference, thanking him for one of the books he had written, *Our Wonderful Jesus.* "I've been going through your little book at my bedtime reading," he wrote, "and I want to commend you for it."

That gracious note prompted my father to write, expressing his appreciation and telling of his plans to see Seventh-day Adventist mission work around the world. Father also expressed the hope that he might be a blessing to those working in distant lands.

That brought a reply and an unexpected offer. "When you get your itinerary all firmed up, send a copy to me. I will write to our leaders where you will be visiting and suggest that they make appointments for you so that you will get to see whatever you wish."

The conference president fulfilled his word by writing many letters of introduction. On each, he penned the words, "Any courtesy and help that you extend to

Brother Tucker and his son will be esteemed a personal favor to me."

Before the trip could be undertaken, a tremendous amount of work had to be done to make sure that the broadcasting ministry would continue uninterrupted. Father worked long hours every night making programs ahead of time that could be played in his absence. *The Quiet Hour* was on twenty-one times each week, and the trip was to last eleven weeks. Thus, 232 half-hour programs had to be made in advance.

I was pastoring in Rochester, New York, at the time, so I flew to New York City and met my father there when he came in from San Francisco. Together we boarded a transatlantic flight and woke up in London. There we found out what a letter from the president of the general conference can do. At the airport, the head of the division greeted Daddy and me as if we were important government officials. They opened their doors and their hearts to us and treated us royally every day.

"It was the same when we landed in France, Germany, and Switzerland," Daddy likes to tell. "The same thing happened in Rome where a young Adventist minister, who had formerly been a Catholic priest, showed us sights that we would not have seen if we had been on our own.

"Everywhere we went, we had speaking opportunities that we could not possibly have arranged by ourselves. We became acquainted with many people and learned of their work in exalting the Lord Jesus."

This trip united father and son in a way that we had

not known before. We had, of course, often prayed together when we were working together in Oakland. But in the Garden of Gethsemane we had an opportunity to pray where the Savior prayed and to walk together where He had walked. On the Isle of Patmos, we knelt down where perhaps the apostle John had knelt when he saw the Lord and received the visions recorded in the Book of Revelation. These experiences molded us together.

Perhaps the highlight of the trip was the visit to Mount Sinai. Daddy tells it this way:

> The president of our work in Egypt, Pastor Neal Wilson, now general conference president, met us at the airport in Cairo and proved to be a great opener of doors. The military was everywhere persent in that country . . . and often we would be stopped at checkpoints. Our host would mumble a few words of Arabic, and we would be permitted to pass on.
>
> Normally single cars were not allowed to drive alone into the desert because of the great dangers of mechanical breakdown or getting lost. Many people died in the hot sun after going for what they thought was just an interesting and short sightseeing trip.
>
> But our host arranged to get a driver who had been up to Mount Sinai many times; and using his influence, he was able to get permission for us to drive out alone. Because of the extreme heat of the day, it was our aim to make most of the trip at night. But it didn't work out. We started out in the

evening, but when we reached the Suez Canal, the man who was supposed to be on duty to sign our pass and allow us to proceed was not there. His wife was having her first baby, and he had left to be on hand.

Yet, we were able to find someone else in authority to give us the required signature. We continued on and crossed the bridge which brought us to the territory that led up to Mount Sinai. However, the man whose signature was needed at that point had gone to bed and wouldn't get up until five.

Sitting all night in a taxi cab can be very uncomfortable, we found out. But at five o'clock in the morning, the man came out, affixed his signature to our pass, and waved us on. With that, we headed down the highway until sunup and came to a stop at the edge of the Red Sea. We gathered a few small sea shells but were hoping to locate one of the wheels that came off Pharaoh's chariots when he and the Egyptians chased the Israelites through that body of water!

From here we left the highway and headed into the desert with no road to follow. At times, we came to places where it seemed like there was no way through the mountains. But, just like it was with the children of Israel, we, too, found the openings and finally reached the great high plain with Mount Sinai ahead on our left.

At the foot of the mountain was St Catherine's monastery. The monks were most gracious to us.

While they couldn't share their meager food supply, they did give us assurance of a place to rest for the night.

We picked up our portable recording equipment, and a monk led us up steps that had been constructed most of the way up the mountain. I can well imagine how an angel might have had to come down and lift Moses over those rocks because they are so impassable.

When, at last, we reached the summit, I had one of the most sacred and solemn experiences of my life. I recalled that when God had come down and spoken the Ten Commandments, that mountain was set on fire. I could see the evidence of the fire where the rocks had melted and congealed.

I remember how that Moses hid in the cleft of the rock as the glory of the Lord passed by. LaVerne and I found a cleft, perhaps the same one, and knelt down for a long season of prayer. We remembered everyone that we could think of by name. And we prayed for members of our radio family.

We recorded a broadcast to be sent back home and played over the stations carrying *The Quiet Hour*. We tried to tell our listeners, as best we could, that society would never be right until it squares itself with Sinai and God's Word. I quoted from the Bible. "And it shall come to pass, if thou shalt hearken diligently unto the voice of the LORD thy God, to observe and to do all his commandments which I command thee this day, then the Lord thy God will set thee on high above all nations of the earth'' (Deut. 28:1).

With a continued sense of the presence of God, my father and I continued our trip around the world. We left the Bible lands and continued on to India and then climaxed our stay among the cannibals of New Guinea. From place to place we sent tapes back to keep *The Quiet Hour* listeners informed as to our progress. And in *The Echoes,* Father wrote detailed accounts of his impressions of each major place we visited.

On this journey, Father and I saw firsthand the tremendous work Adventist missionaries are doing. And we also observed the great need that existed then for technical assistance to enlarge and facilitate their outreach. We didn't know it at the time, but before long we would realize that our enlarged vision of the world would be transmitted to listeners and readers who were able to do something.

12

God, You Are
Just the Same

After this round-the-world tour, Daddy thought his travels were over. But the following year, 1954, God indicated to him that he was to make another pastoral change within the United States, from Oakland to Berrien Springs, Michigan.

Emmanuel Missionary College, now known as Andrews University, needed a chaplain; and although Father, himself, was not a college graduate, they thought Pastor J. L. Tucker could handle the responsibilities well. He would counsel students and also teach one Monday-Wednesday-Friday course per semester in the Bible department. Mrs. Tucker would have a ministry with the women students, which was to prove most effective.

But Chaplain Tucker would have a second, even more demanding responsibility—that of pastoring the College Church. "It was like this," Father explained. "When invited to go to Michigan, I was told by the president of the conference and the president of the college that they had had a church there for forty

103

years, but they had never had a church building. It would be my responsibility to see that an adequate structure was built." So, right from the beginning my father knew it would be his major task to help build a new church sanctuary.

A third concern would lay claim on my father's time. In seventeen years of radio broadcasting, he had prepared and presented more than twelve thousand radio programs, becoming well-known for this ministry in the Portland, Oregon, and the San Francisco Bay areas. So, now the people in Michigan wanted to know if he were going to enter broadcasting in the Midwest.

From a practical standpoint, that would be difficult. Father had completely severed his relationship with the radio work on the West Coast. As he had done when moving from Portland to Berkeley, he had once again left behind everything—office equipment, studio facilities, even a mailing list containing the names of 14,000 contributors. He took with him only the title, *The Quiet Hour*, and the deep, resonant voice that people had come to love and trust.

The possibility of getting back into broadcasting would also be difficult from a philosophical standpoint. After Father's first sermon at the college, all the Adventist ministers of the state of Michigan attended a camp meeting at Grand Lodge.

"Brother Tucker," two local pastors with broadcasts asked, "are you going to do any radio work in Michigan?"

"I don't know," Father replied. "I believe in it. I think every pastor ought to be on the air. I believe that

104

this means of communication was brought into being primarily for the purpose of telling the gospel story."

"Well, don't think that you can get money for such a work here like you did in California," one said. "I've been on the air for eighteen months, and I've never gotten a dollar from the general public. The cost is put in the church budget, and the church cares for it."

The other pastor with a radio program declared that he, too, had never received any money from the public.

Father recognized at once that since his own congregation was about to embark on an expensive building program, he could not seek or expect support from his church. But then, why should that be necessary, he thought. His broadcast ministry had always been entirely supported by the gifts and prayers of those who listened. God was the same in Michigan as on the West Coast.

The conference president agreed that Father could resume his broadcasting, provided he was responsible for getting the money.

On the way home from camp meeting, Father stopped in at Battle Creek and visited several radio stations to see if they would add him to their schedules. But their time was completely sold out.

So, he drove over to Kalamazoo to visit station WKZO. Yes, a half hour was available each week, and the station agreed to sell it to Pastor Tucker and *The Quiet Hour* for thirty dollars. Like Gideon of old, Father decided to put out a fleece to discover if this was really God's will for him to resume broadcasting.

This was to be my test to see if God wanted me back on the air. I prayed this prayer: "Heavenly Father, from this very first broadcast, let me know if you want me to continue. Let me know if this is to be my life's work from here on out. You have heard what the brethren said, that they never received support from the public. But would You send in money from non-Adventist sources as an unmistakable indication that this is Your will?"

Father borrowed a microphone and tape recorder, put together the best program he knew how, and took it to the station for broadcasting. Then, he prayed earnestly and waited expectantly.

On Wednesday following the Sunday broadcast, the mailman stopped by with some letters, perhaps a half dozen. Father eagerly opened the first to see what it might contain. Out came a fifty-dollar bill from a non-Adventist listener.

"My faith went right through the clouds," Father recalls. "I proclaimed, 'God, You are just the same. Now I know You really want me to broadcast!' "

If God could provide the funds for a program on a small-town station, could He not also bring in support for a ministry on a large city outlet? To Father, this seemed perfectly logical and reasonable. So having received the "go" sign from the Lord and being convinced that nothing was too big for God, my daddy decided to seek the best. He drove over to the Detroit area and contracted to buy time each week on the fifty-thousand-watt Canadian radio station serving the area, CKLW. The cost—$240 each week.

News traveled fast, as usual. The next day the

conference president came to visit Father in his home.

"Is it true what I've heard, that you have bought time on CKLW for $240 a week?"

"Yes."

"Now, didn't I tell you plainly when you came to this pastorate that you would be on your own if you wanted to broadcast—that we had no money for radio?"

"Yes."

"Well, whoever heard of a radio pastor receiving $240 from his listeners in one week? You will bring reproach upon yourself, your church and your denomination! I advise you to get back to Detroit as quickly as possible and cancel your contract."

Father asked whether this counsel constituted an order. Then, he went on to explain how he had put out the fleece before the Lord and how God had so clearly answered. He said that he took this as a direct sign that he was to enter the broadcasting field again and that God would supply, no matter how big the need.

The conference official shook his head. "Brother Tucker," he said at last, "I wish I had your faith." Before long, however, this church leader became an enthusiastic supporter of this broadcasting ministry in which God had so evidently led.

In counsel with the conference, it was decided to incorporate *The Quiet Hour* as a nonprofit, religious organization completely separate from any denominational support. Neither was the broadcast identified as being Adventist. People heard the program for what it was, receiving from it spiritual help, instruction, and comfort. Baptists contributed to *The Quiet Hour*, as did Methodists, Presbyterians, Catholics—people from all religious groups.

Adventists, of course, did listen. Sometimes such friends would ask if it was proper for them to devote some of their tithe money to support *The Quiet Hour*. Father would tell them that he never invited such financial help, since he believed the tithe ought to be given to the local church where one held membership. Believing that the denomination ought to be properly supported, Father did not want to drain off funds that should go to local work.

As it turned out, instead of *taking* denominational appropriations, *The Quiet Hour* has *contributed* millions of dollars for Adventist missionary work around the world.

Although Father was starting his radio ministry from scratch, he still published *The Quiet Hour Echoes*, and he kept readers informed about what God was doing. One great advance, made within a month of settling in Berrien Springs, was the decision to release *The Quiet Hour* over two powerful radio stations in Mexico. These stations reached a great area of the United States. Station XEG's one-hundred-thousand-watt voice roared out of Monterey, covering southern, central, and eastern parts of the United States. Blanketing the California and western states, station XERB also served as a mighty voice for *The Quiet Hour*.

In the October, 1954, *Echoes*, Father wrote,

Fellow believers in Christ, pray. Pray that this great venture for Christ will succeed. *The Quiet Hour* is a voice bringing certainty and assurance. It is a voice bringing love, sympathy, and understanding. It is a voice making the truth of God plain, positive, and appealing. It is a voice in the wilderness . . . calling all to come to the Lamb of God Who alone can save to the uttermost.

Listeners to the broadcasts and readers of *The Echoes* responded by sending in gifts for the ministry. Soon Father decided to take another step of faith. He drove over to Chicago and bought time on WLS, a fifty-thousand-watt, clear channel station that at night boomed out to thirty-four central and eastern states, plus provinces of Canada. This first broadcast drew 775 letters.

It is unfortunately true that some broadcasters see radio work as a means of making merchandise of listeners and of personally enriching themselves. Father was determined that no such charge could ever be leveled against him. So, he made a covenant with God that he considers to be the secret of his great success.

"Father, if You will open the doors of opportunity and supply the money through channels of Your own choosing, I will do the work as best I know how and I will never take a penny of remuneration from this radio ministry."

God has proved to be a wonderful partner. Although great amounts of money have been sent in by *The Quiet Hour* listeners and *The Echoes* readers, it has passed through Father's hands and not into them. On resuming his radio work in Michigan, Father lived on his salary as chaplain and pastor. Today, although still heavily involved in broadcasting, he lives on income derived as a retired Adventist pastor of forty-two years and from Social Security. God honors those who honor Him.

The final issue of *The Quiet Hour Echoes* published from Berrien Springs gives this radio log of radio stations:

Chicago, WLS, 890 kc, Sunday, 9 p.m. (C.T.), No. Central U.S.

Detroit, CKLW, 800 kc, Sunday, 8:30 p.m. (E.T.), Northeast U.S.

Philadelphia, WNAR, 1110 kc, Sunday, 8:30 a.m.

Kalamazoo, WKZO, 590 kc, Sunday 9 a.m. (E.T.), Michigan

San Antonio, XEG, 1050 kc, Saturday, 10 p.m. (C.T.), C. and So. States

San Diego, XERB, 1090 kc, Sunday, 8 p.m. (P.T.), So. Calif. Daily, 6:30 a.m. (P.T.), So. Calif.

St. Johns, VOAR, 1230 kc, Sunday, 2:30 p.m. (E.T.), Newfoundland

Boise, KIDO, 1410 kc, Monday through Friday, 4:30 p.m. Monday, 7:30 a.m., Kansas City area

Shenandoah, KMA, 960 kc, Sunday, 8 p.m. (C.T.), Iowa, Neb., Kans., Mo.

Leavenworth, KCLO, 1410 kc, Monday through Friday, 4:30 p.m. Monday, 7:30 a.m., Kansas City area

Portland, KWJJ, 1080 kc, Monday through Friday, 9:30 p.m., Northwest U.S.

Despite his heavy broadcast involvement, Father gave primary attention to his work as chaplain and pastor of the College Church. He assumed the position as chairman of the building committee and helped raise more than three hundred thousand dollars toward the construction of a beautiful stone church, seating twenty-one hundred. Father looks today with warm sentiment at a color photograph of this building, because he poured into it so much of his love and labor.

After five and a half years of service to the college, the church, and *The Quiet Hour*, father had passed the time at which Adventists pastors may officially retire and go fishing. Could it be that his life's ministry was now to come to a close at the age of sixty-four? Or did God have something further in mind that would make the future even more glorious and productive than the past?

13

Is There Life After Retirement?

As anyone who has ever done it knows, moving from the mild climate of the West Coast to the harsh winters of the upper Midwest can be a shock. For almost eleven years, my father and mother had lived in California, and they had all but forgotten what it was like to live where the snow piles up by the foot and the wind howls through barren trees.

The change proved difficult for my mother, who had seldom enjoyed robust health. Eventually, the time came, after four hard winters in Berrien Springs, that my mother was advised by her family physicians to move to a warmer part of the country.

But where? The mild and dry climate of southern California around Redlands seemed ideal. By this time, Daddy had served the denomination for forty-one years, more than enough to officially retire; and yet he felt that his work as college chaplain and as pastor in Michigan was not completed. So, he requested Mother to move to California and survey the land while he continued to tie up loose ends.

In the warm, sunny climate where vegetable and fruit farming continues year round, Mother's health began to improve. It was a matter of deep thanksgiving to God.

But living as a bachelor proved a difficult assignment for Daddy. After all, he had enjoyed the love and companionship of his wife for four decades. He missed the touch of her hand, the sound of her voice, her counsel and advice relating to his pastoral work and broadcasting.

Finally, Father decided to officially retire from his active pastorate and to devote himself exclusively to his radio ministry. "I wrote to Ida and told her she'd better buy a house out there where it agreed with her and that I'd be out as soon as possible."

It wasn't easy for the college and church to say goodbye to Pastor Tucker that fall in 1959, the close of his five and a half years of happy association. They had come to love him greatly, as had the people in other places where he had served. A "This Is Your Life" presentation proved an emotional time for all.

As usual, Pastor Tucker of the radio ministry, kept his *Echoes* readers aware of what was happening. To them he wrote,

Yes, it's moving time again. Moving is one of the experiences of the minister. Truly, we say with the song writer that we have no abiding city here . . . Through our ministry it seems every move gets a little harder to make, the ties of friendship and love become sweeter and closer, but we have the blessed assurance that each move brings us nearer to that wonderful day of homegoing to our Father's house. I have often thought that when I reach that heavenly city, I'd put up a sign by the side of the house, "DONE MOVING."

To show its appreciation for his ministry, the conference where Pastor Tucker was leaving arranged for and paid the cost for two trucks to bring my father's and mother's possessions to Redlands, California. Daddy drove the family car and eagerly looked forward to arriving at 1017 La Cresta Drive, the home Mother had purchased but which Father had never seen. This time he brought along all things pertaining to his radio broadcasting, since his outreach had been personal rather than denominational. He intended to continue his broadcasting service in retirement.

The large house proved ideal for their needs because it became not only a home but the center for *The Quiet Hour*. The dining room, for example, became the place where the mail was sorted and answered. Every room, except the bedroom, was pressed into service. Even the garage became a part of the broadcasting operation. I know this from personal observation and participation—on the way out to the Philippines for missionary service, I stopped by and helped build needed shelving. For the next ten years, *The Quiet Hour* offices again were in the home of the speaker.

It was a new experience to be unassigned by a conference—to be retired with no pastorate. But with excellent health and enthusiasm, Father was anxious to get the broadcast established on more stations, both locally and across the country. Though there were many obstacles, once again Father discovered that his personal philosophy evolved over the years served him well: Keep sweet—keep smiling—keep stepping.

Immediately there was evidence of divine guidance as the self-supporting ministry began to slowly but firmly expand. New members from southern California were added to the board of directors. The conference volunteered to annually audit the financial records, and to this day everything has always been found in perfect order.

By the time the twenty-fifth anniversary of *The Quiet Hour* had come along in July, 1962, the broadcast was being carried on thirty-five stations across the country, many of them powerful outlets, having potential audiences of millions of people. In *The Echoes,* my father wrote, "The service we have rendered has never grown old. Long hours are shortened as we sense more fully the value of the souls that are touched by this influence and are brought to a full surrender to God."

Father was now sixty-seven years old, past the time when most men are phasing out an active life and beginning to ease up. But now "in retirement" he was working as hard as ever.

Part of the expansion of *The Quiet Hour* ministry was due to an increased emphasis on missions. An annual missions month called the attention of listeners and readers to special projects that could be met through regular and sacrificial giving. One of the most urgent requests involved transportation for Adventist missionaries working in New Guinea. The problem could largely be solved through the gift of an airplane to fly personnel and equipment into remote areas that took weeks of hard travel by foot to reach. So the need was made known, and in 1965 an airplane was sent out for service.

Before long, the results of this gift became apparent. One of four pilots using the aircraft, a pastor named Barnard, wrote an informative letter that was published in *The Echoes*. In part, it reads:

The amount of extra work we are able to do now is astonishing, and I often sit back myself and marvel at what is accomplished every week. But what is most thrilling is the way the whole area is opening up with literally hundreds upon hundreds scrambling to get into the baptismal classes. I will be baptizing over a hundred in this section alone. Wonderful things are happening here in backward New Guinea at this time. This land of savages is stirring as never before, and God will have many precious jewels from this dark land.

Such encouraging reports were more than enough to generate interest in other projects to provide airplanes for missionaries. A second aircraft was sent out to New Guinea, then more to other fields. As many as five planes were sent out at one time, and over the years the total has exceeded fifty. It is impossible to estimate the tremendous impact on missions that has been made possible through the faithful giving of *The Quiet Hour* listeners and *Echoes* readers.

The time came when the growing outreach of *The Quiet Hour* could no longer be handled from the ten-room Tucker home. The growing staff found it difficult to find parking places on the streets. A friend of the ministry made a vacant building available, which became the headquarters for the next five years.

Twelve years after father had "retired," *The Quiet Hour* was being carried on 150 stations. Father might justly have been proud of this great accomplishment; yet, he wrote to *Echoes* readers of the dangers of the disease of "The Minimum." Instead, he called for "The Maximum" in faith and endeavor, urging his friends to pray, "Lord, make all there is of me and all You can make of me." The evidence of this prayer is eminently apparent in Daddy's own life.

In summarizing the impact of *The Quiet Hour* after a ministry of more than three decades, Father expressed himself this way:

Radio cannot be used effectively and successfully in soul-winning and as a self-supporting agency without a firm faith that God wants you to do it and that it can be done. The glamour of radio soon wears off, but the joy that comes in the consciousness of being a voice for God—that souls are reborn, that backsliders are reclaimed, that the saints are more securely anchored, all this—grows with every passing day.

At the annual meetings of *The Quiet Hour* Board of Directors in 1969 and 1970, it was emphasized that the time had come for the father and son team to be reunited. There was also need for a stronger follow-up ministry to be organized, and the Board requested that I leave my pastoral work and unite full-time with my father in making *The Quiet Hour* ministry more productive.

At this time, I was pastoring a church in Chattanooga, Tennessee, and engaged in a vibrant radio and television ministry that was touching the lives of thousands. Five times a day, our three-minute radio program entitled *Call to Prayer* was released. Our twice-daily telecast was also released under the same title on the CBS affiliate, WDEF-TV, channel 12. Both the radio and television programs were public service.

Because of the public demand for a longer telecast, a half-hour program called *Search* was developed and released every Sunday morning at 9:30. The name was chosen from heaven's wonderful promise, "And ye shall seek me and find me when ye shall search for me with all your heart" (Jer. 29:13).

Originally there was to be a charge for the air time for this telecast of seventy-five dollars a program, but after viewing the first one, the manager of the station said, "Pastor Tucker, I appreciated so much the warmth of your ministry. There will be no charge for that half-hour program." This was a good sign that God was blessing this telecast ministry. When we accepted the invitation of *The Quiet Hour* board to join hands with my dear father, we brought the *Search* telecast right along with us, and it has become a very important part of *The Quiet Hour* worldwide ministry, with weekly telecasts released in the Philippines on ten stations and on more than fifty stations in North America.

Arriving in Redlands in August, 1971, I said to my father, "Daddy, I'm here to be your support. I've not come to take your place. I want you to keep on working as hard as you choose to. One thing for sure, I don't want you to sit in a rocking chair and just rock.

Set your own pace. Whenever you say that you're tired, just go home and rest." But you know, it's hard to get Daddy to slow down. True, he gets tired, but with a couple of naps a day and a good night's rest, he seems to accomplish more than any man I've ever known. And he's in his mid-eighties!

What a joy it is as we join hands together and bow our hearts in praise and petition to our God to see *The Quiet Hour* ministry growing more and more each year. The number of radio stations carrying *The Quiet Hour* has risen from 150 in 1971 to 450 released per week currently. The goal of having 500 stations is readily at hand. With this growth came the necessity of moving to more spacious headquarters. A building was spotted with a "For Sale" sign at 630 Brookside, at the corner of Center, near the heart of town. After some needed remodeling and the building of a warehouse, we moved to our current address, and our large lot offers room for future expansion.

As director and principal speaker of *The Quiet Hour*, my father comes into his office almost every day and works solidly through until noon. Then, he gets in his 1969 Pontiac and drives the two miles to home where he has lunch. Next, in his own words, he "meditates in the horizontal" an hour or so (others would call it sleeping), after which he returns to the office at about 3:00 and stays until 5:30 before going home for the day.

Some day, the Lord will call Father to another home, to an eternal home in heaven. He longs to see it and has helped prepare many thousands of others to go there through his remarkable sixty-two years of ministry.

At the beginning of this project of telling his life's story, Father said, "It could be entitled *Life Has Been Wonderful,* for that's exactly what is has been. God has been gracious and has given so many blessings. I hope the account of my journey will be to His glory."

Father has always had a deep appreciation for the value of a soul purchased by the blood of Jesus Christ. It seems like every energy of his life has been devoted to bringing blessing to others, helping people to see their true value as it is in Christ Jesus. One of his favorite promises has brought warmth, challenge, and encouragement to so many thousands: "He raiseth up the poor out of the dust, and lifteth up the beggar from the dunghill, to set them among princes, and to make them inherit the throne of glory" (1 Sam. 2:8).

As Father would seek to point someone to Jesus and help that one see his true value, I've heard him say,

God wants you and every living soul to recapture the grand design that He had for man in the beginning. He wants to awaken in your mind and heart the glorious truth that you, too, were designed for greatness.

The trouble is too many people are living in a dunghill, in the dust, and they're glad to be there. They've lost their vision. They don't understand. Somehow there must be rekindled in their minds this vision of the throne and the glory of greatness that God has in mind for man. Too many are living in the dunghill in their thoughts, words, and deeds. They live amongst the filth and dirt. They may have their names on the church books, but they are living on that low, dunghill level. God wants to get you out of the dunghill and put you on a throne. You were designed not for dust or dunghill, but for a throne and for greatness.

When you're tempted to be discouraged and to speak and act like those who are on that low, base level, I wish the vision could come—"I belong to a throne!"

Read and reread this passage, and remember that Jesus came to raise up "the poor out of the dust and lift up the beggar from the dunghill, to set them among princes and to make them inherit the throne of glory." Yes, you were designed for royalty. You are a prince or a princess of the kingdom of God! He has now designed you to inherit the throne of glory. That's where you belong if you only knew it. That's where God wants you to be!

APPENDIX

GIVE GOD A CHANCE

New stations begin carrying The Quiet Hour *each week. The first broadcast in each new series includes a message by my father entitled "Give God a Chance." I thought you would like to share it.*

Over in London, some time ago, a noble woman died. God touched her eyes, and they were closed; her heart, and it ceased its beating. They carried her into one of the greatest auditoriums so that the city and the world might pay her honor. A representative of the Queen honored her by being present. Lords and ladies were there; the rich people of England came to look and weep. At last the poor people came pressing their way into the great building. The weeping thousands passed beside the sleeping woman.

At last a very poor woman made her way down the aisle. She had every mark of poverty; she carried a child on one arm, and led another by the hand. When she reached the coffin, she put the baby on the floor, loosed the clasp of the other child's hand, and then stooped to kiss the glass which covered the face, thereby stopping the passing of the throng. The guard, stepping forward, took her by the shoulder, saying as he did so: "Woman, you will have to move on; you are stopping the people." She lifted her face to his for a moment, and then, turning to the surging mass of people in the building, she cried out: "My friends, I will not move on! I have walked sixty miles, and carried my baby, that I might look upon this woman's face. She saved my boys from hell, and I have a right to look and to weep." Then bending down she kissed again and again the glass covering the face, while the multitude sobbed in sympathy with her.

Who was she, sleeping in the coffin yonder? Why, that was Mrs. Booth, the mother of the Salvation Army, one of the grandest women God has ever called into His service.

This noble woman gave God a chance to bless multitudes. She was not great because of nobility or rank, or because she possessed material prosperity or an unusual amount of genius and talent, but because she gave her all in consecrated service to the needy. She let go and let God work through her. Like Paul of old she could say, "For me to live is Christ."

Today God is looking for lives that He can make channels of blessing to a perishing world. He says, "Prove Me and I will open the windows of heaven; give Me a chance and see what I can do for you and through you." Heaven's windows are not boarded up. The bolts are not rusty. God opened the windows of blessing for Moses when he wholly trusted God, and the Red Sea parted. He opened the window for Joshua, and old Jordan rolled back. He opened the same windows for Gideon, and his trusting, zealous three hundred saw the hosts of the enemy flee. It has always been the same through the ages. God has not changed. He is the same yesterday, today, and forever (Heb. 13:8). "I am the LORD, I change not" (Mal. 3:6). To the man of faith the windows of heaven are kept oiled and ready to swing wide open.

Give God a Chance by Believing

Faith is the soul's intake. Faith gives God a chance. Faith is a bridge over the chasm of despair on which the loads of heaven's blessing ride earthward. Unbelief is at the root of all failure—all sin—all weakness. Unbelief is like cotton in your ears so you can't hear. It's like bandages over your eyes so you can't see. Coming to God in unbelief is like holding a corked bottle under the faucet. Before anything fine and glorious can fill our lives, unbelief must go out. A little child defined faith in this way: "It's taking God at His word and asking no questions."

Little Mary stood on the kitchen floor,
Gazing down at the old trap door
Into the cellar dark and damp.
She could only see a tiny lamp
At her papa's side;
She knew he was there,
For she saw him herself go down the stair;
And now and then she could hear him speak,

Though the voice seemed far away and weak.
"Papa," she called in her baby tone,
"Are you there, dear Papa? I am all alone."
"Why, yes, little daughter, be sure I am here;
Jump and I'll catch you, do not fear."
"Where are you, Papa? Do come to me."
"No, daughter, jump; I will hold you fast,
Come now!" and Mary jumped at last.
He held her trembling in close embrace,
And pressed a kiss on her baby face,
While a simple lesson the child he taught,
A lesson she never in life forgot:
"My dear, that's the way to obey the Lord;
Though you cannot see Him, believe in His Word.
He will say, 'Here I am,' to every call.
Trust Him, He never will let you fall."

The reason men are not saved is because they won't trust God. They won't give Him a chance. We take our watch to the watchmaker and leave it wholly in his hands. We take our car to the garageman and trust it to his ability and care. We give them a chance. Why not give God a chance to do something for time and eternity for these hearts and lives of ours so marred by sin? We must not wait in giving God a chance until our faith is big and perfect. It will grow.

There was once a good woman who was well-known for her simple faith and great calmness in the midst of many trials. Another woman living at a distance, hearing of her said, "I must go and see that woman and learn the secret of her calm, happy life." She went and, accosting the woman, said, "Are you the woman with the great faith?" "No," was the answer, "I am not the woman with the great faith, but I am the woman with a little faith in the great God."

We please God when we trust Him. We grieve Him with our unbelief. "Without faith it is impossible to please him" (Heb. 11:6). "He that believeth not God hath made him a liar" (1 John 5:10). Faith depends wholly on God's Word. "Faith cometh by hearing, and hearing by the word of God" (Rom. 10:17). Faith does not take counsel of fears and circumstances when once God has spoken. As an illustration of this we have the story of Paul enroute to Rome by ship. The devil is determined to sink the boat and destroy the passengers, especially Paul. What a storm! (Read the story in Acts 27.) Those hardy seamen had never battled with such odds. They did everything humanly possible, but soon "all hope was gone," from every heart except Paul's. After fourteen days and nights of being battered by the tempest, with the old boat pitching and tossing, with the howl of the hurricane in his ears, with the salt spray in his face, but with faith in his heart, Paul cries,

. . . There stood by me this night the angel of God, whose I am, and whom I serve, Saying, Fear not, Paul; thou must be brought before Caesar: and lo, God hath given thee all them that sail with thee. Wherefore, sirs, be of good cheer: for I believe God, that it shall be even as it was told me.

And it was. Had Paul been looking only at circumstances he would have been as the other 275 passengers, but he counted on God's good word of promise which cannot be broken or fail (John 10:35; 1 Kings 8:56).

Give God a Chance by Praying

"Ask, and ye shall receive" (John 16:24). "Call upon me, and I will answer" (Ps. 91:15). "Prayer . . . availeth much" (James 5:16). There are many things we cannot do, but God says, If you ask, I will do. There are burdens too heavy to bear. There are problems too knotty to solve, but there is nothing too high to scale; there is nothing too hard for God. Jeremiah's trust can be our confidence. "Ah Lord Gᴏᴅ! behold, thou hast made the heaven and the earth by thy great power and stretched out arm, and there is nothing too hard for thee" (Jer. 32:17). "Call unto me, and I will answer thee, and shew thee great and mighty things, which thou knowest not" (Jer. 33:3). Our part is to call; God's part is to answer and show great and mighty things. True, we must call in faith; we must call in the will of God; we must call in singleness of purpose; we must call with hearts reaching out for God. We must call for the glory of His name and cause. We must call in Jesus' name. But we **must** call. We **must** pray. "If my people, which are called by my name, shall humble themselves, and pray, and seek my face, . . . then will I hear from heaven, and will forgive their sin, and will heal their land" (2 Chron. 7:14). And then He adds these encouraging words: "Now mine eyes shall be open, and mine ears attent unto the prayer that is made" (v. 15).

Pray when the storm clouds gather o'er head,
Hiding the light from you;
Filling your soul with darkness and dread,
Pray 'till the light breaks through.

Pressed under sorrow, near to despair;
Troubles, your soul pursue;
Go to your Father, tell Him your care,
Pray 'till the light breaks through.

Pray then believing, God on the throne,
Looks with compassion true;
Unto His children, cares for His own,
Pray 'till the light breaks through.

Give God a Chance by Patiently Waiting

We must be patient as we wait upon God in prayer, for it may take time for Him to bring about the answer. He takes time to paint a rose, to grow an oak, or to make a loaf of bread from the grains sown in the field. We pray for a loved one's conversion and ofttimes wonder why things don't happen at once. Give God a chance by patiently waiting and resting in assurance; the answer will come. Do not become impatient if you see no change immediately in the life and attitude of the one for whom you pray. God must move upon their will. Heart idols will have to be overthrown; cherished plans will have to be foiled. It may take affliction, bereavement, and sickness. God will have to woo, to disappoint, to enrich or impoverish, to unstop deaf ears, to open blind eyes, to turn aside wandering feet; and it takes time.

Daniel is known as one of God's noblest, wisest, and most devoted saints. He knew what it was to have instant answers to prayer (Dan. 9:20,21). He knew what it was to have to wait. After weeks of waiting on God, the angel came with the explanation:

Fear not, Daniel: for from the first day that thou didst set thine heart to understand, and to chasten thyself before thy God, thy words were heard, and I am come for thy words. But the prince of the kingdom of Persia withstood me one and twenty days: but, lo, Michael, one of the chief princes, came to help me; and I remained there with the kings of Persia. Now I am come to make thee understand (Dan. 10:12–14).

Some years ago I had the blessed privilege of baptizing a man whose good wife had been praying earnestly, believingly, perseveringly, prevailingly for him for thirty-nine years. There is a motto that reads, "You can do more than pray **after** you have prayed, but you cannot do more than pray **until** you have prayed."

Thoughts on Prayer

"Prayer is the key in the hand of faith that unlocks heaven's storehouse."

"To ask God to give to us when we refuse to give to His work is not praying; it is just idle talk."

"We have no right to ask God to do things for us when we are refusing to do things for Him."

"Prayer is the opening of the heart to God as to a friend."

"The effectual fervent prayer of a righteous man availeth much" (James 5:16).

"A great many people go to church praying that they may hear preaching that will hit somebody else."

"Some people pray for dying grace, when what they need most is grace to make them *live* within their means and pay their debts."

Give God a Chance by Yielding

He can do nothing for us unless we yield to Him. Before He can impower, He must possess. In the early days of his struggle toward truth, Augustine made a prayer, "Lord, save me from my sins but not quite yet." Then sometime after that, he prayed, "Lord, save me from all my sins except one." And then came the final prayer, "Lord, save me from all my sins and save me **now**." It was when he made the full and complete surrender that the victory was his.

When someone asked a ruler of Brazil years ago how he explained the backwardness of his country, he said it was due to "Mañana." What does it mean? "Tomorrow." Wherever a person or a people goes on saying "Mañana," there is no hurry; there is plenty of time; there you have found degeneracy and decay and death. "Tomorrow" is a fool's paradise; it is a mirage; it is the devil's anesthetic to deaden our consciences. God calls for a full surrender **now**—today. "Behold, now is the day of salvation" (2 Cor. 6:2). Not argument, but surrender. Not debate, but obedience. Not delay, but **now.**

The cause of our barren, unfruitful lives is our failure to yield to the control of the Holy Spirit. Moses, with stammering tongue, yielded, thus giving God a chance. Gideon was fearful, but he yielded to God's commands and gave God a chance to manifest His power. David was but a stripling, but his surrendered life became a channel through which God could work. The unknown boy who followed the crowd to hear Jesus had only a lunch, but he surrendered it, thus giving Jesus a chance, and thousands were blessed because of it. Seven weary fishermen toiled all night with no success, but upon yielding to Jesus' word, "Cast your net on the right side," there was a wonderful catch.

Another time Peter had worked through the hours of the night with no fruitage and was wearily cleaning his nets, when Jesus came and said, "Launch out into the deep and let down your net." For a moment Peter thought to argue the futility of such an idea. It was daybreak—successful fishing was done on that lake by night. Peter reminded Jesus that they had toiled all night and taken nothing, but he quickly adds a note of yieldedness, "Nevertheless at thy word I will let down the net" (Luke 5:5). When he gave Jesus a chance by yielding, what a difference; the catch was more than his net could take.

All God asks is a chance. Your talents may be few; your ability limited; it matters not. Yield what you have. God can work miracles with little if the little is surrendered—dedicated. If we will be yielded clay in the hands of the divine potter, He will mold us into vessels of use and for His glory.

Dear reader, will you please write and tell us that from now on you will give God a chance in and through your life? He is the only one that is able to meet the needs of your soul. He alone can direct doubting, halting hearts to the pathway of peace. In Him alone is the secret of victory and keeping power.

Believe Him! Pray to Him! Wait upon Him! Yield completely to Him, and you will be amazed at the new meaning life has. I'll be anxiously looking for your letter of decision.

J. L. Tucker
The Quiet Hour
Redlands, Calif. 92373

WRITINGS OF J. L. TUCKER

Besides being the editor of The Echoes *for all these years, J. L. has written the following booklets and books.*

Short Pamphlets

All This and Heaven Too
Be Not Afraid
Five Centuries of Prophecies Fulfilled in One Day
Fundamentals of Faith
Give God a Chance
God Has a Plan for Your Life
God or Evolution?
He Cares
Heaven and Our Eternal Home
The Heavenly View
How Can I Be Ready for Christ's Coming?
Just Being Happy
Prayer—the Key in the Hand of Faith
Repent Now!
Salvation Free to All
Selected Gems of Thought
The Bible—God's Word to Man
The Church—God's Last Message To It
The Eleventh Commandment
The Gospel of Good Health
The Lord Is Coming
The Man You Must Know
These Seventh-Day Adventists
Time Is Running Out
Weighed and Found Wanting
What a Gift!
What Jesus Is to Me
When Days Are Dark
When God Said Remember

Longer Pamphlets

Angels and Their Ministry

Appendix

Bones in the Church
Building a Happy Home
Elijah—the Man for This Crisis Hour
God in the Shadows
God's Holy Things
How Are the Mighty Fallen
I Walked Where Jesus Walked
It Happened at Night
Jesus
John—A Man Sent from God
In the Beginning God
Looking Unto Jesus
Maintaining a Christian Experience
Our Lord's Return
Our Wonderful Bible
Quiet Hour Talks
Revelation Beatitudes of Jesus
Some Absolute Essentials in Christian Experience
The Beast and His Mark
The Devil and His Devices
The Great I Am
The King Is Coming
The Man Who Tried to Run Away from God
The Master and His Friends
Your Questions Answered from the Bible
What a Man!
Women to Be Remembered

Books

Another Look at the Christian Sabbath
I Climbed Mt. Sinai
God's Great Questions to Man
Our Wonderful Jesus
Quiet Hour Sermons
Study Notes on the Book of Daniel
Study Notes on the Book of Revelation
The Gospel and What It Saves Us From
The Lord Is My Shepherd
When a Man Dies, What Then?
Wonders of Bible Prophecy

From Dust to Glory

These few poems by my father were written fifty years ago to Ida Jane while he was holding evangelistic meetings in New Mexico. Lonesome and homesick for the ones he loved most, he penned these lines and never saw them again until just recently. In going through some of Ida's things, he found a small box tied up with a ribbon and upon opening it found old letters and these poems she had kept all these years.

MY FLOWER—IDA

There's a garden of flowers, a lovely spot
    Where the roses, violets, and forget-me-nots,
With beauty and fragrance do their part
    To gladden a world and cheer heavy hearts
Along life's way.

In the garden of love sweet flowers bloom;
    They blossom sometimes into a bride and groom.
The flower I found in this garden fair
    To me has a grace and beauty rare
That no other flower had.

You'd blush, I am sure, if I'd confess
    Though I am almost sure that you can guess
That the sweetest flower that ever grew
    In the garden of love was you.
Just you.

You're my rose, bluebell, and violet too,
    My forget-me-not, for you're always true.

You're my zinnia, my lily, also my pick,
   Of daisies and pansies a bouquet, I think
And still you are more.

TRIBUTE TO MUMSEY

If all the coal were diamonds
   And every inch were a mile,
They could not measure the value
   I place on your winning smile.

If all the rain drops were notes
   And the blades of grass were words,
They could not express the music
   Or the joy that your love affords.

If every pebble became a pearl
   And slaves the king of klans
They still could not begin to know
   The honor of being your man.

When every ounce becomes a ton
   And every match a sun,
Then in telling the worth of the girl I have
   I am sure I've just begun.

If thoughts could fill my mind like the surging sea,
   And words fail not as the day,
Then could I express to the one I love best
   That she means the world to me.

MY OWN THREE

I'm thinking of home, for I'm lonesome today.
  I'm longing for loved ones that are miles away.
Am I foolish about them? Don't answer me "yea."
  Be it foolish or wisdom, I feel just that way.

There's "Wan" our first born, his daddy's delight.
  What a treasure God gave us to make our home bright.
We prayed for him earnestly, waiting with joy;
  And the thrill, we can't tell it, when the doctor said, "He's
a boy."

But as the first home in Eden so fair
  Needed the feminine presence to share.
So we needed a Jewell and we got a priceless pearl.
  She's our sunshine—we love her—our sweet smiling girl.

Now "Mumsey" don't scoff nor think I am lying,
  For in this fourth verse I only am trying
To tell you in words that are true—gospel truth—
  The one I need and love most is the wife of my youth.

THE BRAVE YOUNG PREACHER

The young preacher faced the stolid crowd.
  He shook like one of old
Whose drunken feast stopped and despair began
  When God has doom foretold.

His lips became as dry as Gilboa's top
　At the end of the long, long drought;
His tongue became far too big
　For the cavity called a month.

His vision blurred as tho a heavy fog
　Had settled down just then;
And the perspiration started from a million pores
　You'd have thought he'd been in the rain.

His hands and feet got in the way;
　His brain failed to function at all.
His ego is dead; there's only one dread
　That he through a knothole might fall.

O pity the poor, young preacher;
　Encourage him all you can,
For he's a martyr and more—a hero
　Who can thus die—yet try again.

OUR GOD OF LOVE

In awe I gazed at the starlit sky,
　And like one of old I, too, wondered why
That the omnipotent One who cannot die
　Should ever think of man.

His works are so vast and man so small,
　As if a drop from the ocean should fall.
Yet He hears and heeds the faintest call,
　Because He is God.

From Dust to Glory

Tho in awe I gaze at the stars so grand,
  And marvel in wonder at the power of His hand,
Yet His love is the hardest to understand
  How could He love me?

But in the Bible, God's Holy Book,
  If man would only pause and look,
Is the record true of the price it took
  In saving guilty man.

It took the chiefest the universe knew
  To ransom the lost—me and you;
And God our Father was willing, too,
  Because of His love.

Oh sons of men, where e're you be
  Accept His love so full and free
That you might live through eternity
  With our God of love.

Tarry Awhile

COPYRIGHT, 1941, BY J. L. TUCKER

J. L. Tucker

Marjorie Lewis Lloyd

1. I came to the Sav-iour, my life on-ly dross, Claim-ing His prom-ise, ac-
2. Why go on in de-feat when there's vict'ry for you? Why lone-ly be? You've a
3. God sees all the sorrow that's breaking your heart, Dark clouds of an-guish He'll

cept - ing the cross; In His blood I was washed as I talked with Him there;
Friend that is true; And not for a mo-ment need an-y de-spair,
cause to de-part; For He cares when your sin drives you on to de-spair,

CHORUS

I have hope in my heart since I tar-ried in prayer.
There's a store-house of bless-ing, 'tis o-pened by prayer. Tar-ry a-while, O soul
And He'll come to your side as you tar-ry in prayer.

bur-dened with care, Wait at the feet of the Mas-ter in prayer; Your cares will be

lift - ed, On Him they'll be shift-ed, If you tar-ry a-while in prayer.

141

THE CALLING CHRIST

J. L. Tucker

Marjorie Lewis Lloyd

1. From the high-lands of glo-ry a voice called my name, Say-ing
2. 'Twas the call of the Mas-ter God's own pre-cious Son, Who had
3. He is call-ing for you, friend, He pass-es none by; Can't you

Why will you stay in your fol-ly and shame? Leave the way of de-struc-tion,
bat-tled the foe and the vic-to-ry won. He_ of-fers to par-don,
hear His sweet voice com-ing down from the sky? For_ you are so pre-cious,

and "Come un-to Me", For_ why will you per-ish, when life is so free?
to cleanse ev-'ry stain, And to make us a ves-sel of use once a-gain.
so dear to His heart, Yield to-day to His call e'er the Spir-it de-part.

CHORUS

Call-ing, call-ing, call-ing o'er and o'er your name, Call-ing, call-ing,

call-ing, must He call in vain? Tho' He's pa-tient, do not ling-er;

heed it while you may. For the Christ won't plead for-ev-er, but He calls to-day.

WHAT WILL IT BE TO BE THERE

J. L. Tucker

Marjorie Lewis Lloyd

Duet

1. When we gath-er at last by life's riv-er,＿Walk the streets of that
2. We shall meet the re-deemed of all a-ges,＿From the first to the
3. But the chief of the glo-ries of heav-en＿Will be Je-sus our

ci-ty so fair,＿When we dwell in those beau-ti-ful man-sions＿Oh!＿
rem-nant of time,＿Tell the sto-ry of how He redeemed us＿Then＿
Sav-iour to see;＿Just to dwell ev-er more in His pres-ence＿Will be

CHORUS

what will it be to be there!＿
join in the chor-us sub-lime!＿When we gath-er at last ov-er
glo-ry un-end-ing for me!＿

yon-der＿ By the side of the Jor-dan so fair,＿We shall look in the

face of the Mas-ter,＿ And what will it be to be there!＿

143